POP ART

POP ART

Jamie James

For David Fratkin – inspired artist, great friend

Phaidon Press Limited
Regent's Wharf, All Saints Street, London N1 9PA

First published 1996
Reprinted 1998
© Phaidon Press Limited 1996

A CIP catalogue record for this book is available from the
British Library

ISBN 0 7148 3332 0

Printed in Singapore

Cover illustrations:
Front: Andy Warhol. *Marilyn*, 1967 (Plate 34)
Back: Peter Blake. *On the Balcony*, 1955–7 (Plate 5)

The publishers would like to thank all those museum authorities and
private owners who have kindly provided material for use in this publi-
cation. Particular acknowledgement is made for the following: Fig. 13:
British Film Institute, London; Plates 19, 20, 26, 32: Leo Castelli Photo
Archives; Plate 17: Joe Goode Studios; Fig. 25: Marian Goodman
Gallery, New York; Plates 45, 46, Fig. 18: The Estate of Keith Haring;
Plates 14, 15: © David Hockney; Plate 48, Fig. 29: Deborah Kass; Plate
4: Jeff Koons; Plate 36: Collection Bruce R Lewin; Plates 6, 9, 28, 29,
33: Rheinisches Bildarchiv, Cologne; Plate 16, Fig. 6: Statens
Konstmuseer, Stockholm; Plate 12: Centre National d'Art et de
Culture Georges Pompidou, Paris; Fig. 26: Courtesy Billy Name; Plate
8: Courtesy Allan Stone Gallery, New York; Plate 44: Courtesy Tony
Shafrazi Gallery, New York.

Note: All dimensions of works are given height before width before
depth.

Pop Art

For as long as there have been people putting art on a pedestal, there have been others, usually artists themselves, who have taken delight in pulling it off again. Even when Phidias (fl. *c* 490–430 BC) and Praxiteles (fl. *c* 370–330 BC) were producing their exquisite sculptures in ancient Greece, images of gods that were mounted on real pedestals, there were other, nameless sculptors turning out crude Dionysiac trinkets to amuse the masses. In the Romantic era, French artists such as Millet (1814–75) and Daumier (1808–79), and English painters like Stubbs (1724–1806) and Wright of Derby (1734–97), based their art on the proposition that the mundane concerns of everyday life – the working grind of the peasant and the foibles of the petite bourgeoisie, the farmer's livestock and the machines of industry – were a proper subject for art.

Then, in 1917, Marcel Duchamp (1887–1968) turned a porcelain urinal on its side and exhibited it as a sculpture, and two years later he painted a moustache on a postcard of the *Mona Lisa* (Fig. 1). Dada was launched, and it proved to be the most radical anti-art art movement in history. Yet Dada eventually transformed itself into Surrealism, which, for all its emphasis on psychosexuality and bizarre juxtapositions, was nonetheless an art movement in the conventional mould: even the most outrageous fantasies of Miró (1893–1983) and Dali (1904–89) look quite at home in gilded frames.

The true, anarchic strain of Dada did not reassert itself again until the years after World War II, when Pop Art emerged in Great Britain and the United States. Loosely defined, Pop Art is painting and sculpture which borrows its imagery from the mass culture – high art mimicking low art. Thus commercial products, advertisements, newspaper clippings, even comic books and pornography, are fair game for the Pop artist, who elevates these vulgar materials to the status of 'high-brow' culture. The first stirrings of Pop Art were in London, where a group of young artists had grown restive at the lofty ideals and restrictive attitudes which prevailed in the art establishment at that time. In the late 1940s, the Scottish artist Eduardo Paolozzi (1924–) began making satirical collages, using clippings from American newspapers and magazines. In many of them, he made absurd juxtapositions of risqué photographs from girlie and body-building magazines with images of American mass-consumer products, such as automobiles and soda bottles. In 1952, Paolozzi and a group of like-minded young artists and critics, which included Richard Hamilton (1922–), Nigel Henderson, Lawrence Alloway (1926–) and Reyner Banham, began to meet informally at the Institute of Contemporary Arts in London. Calling themselves the Independent Group, they echoed Dadaism by challenging the notion that art had a claim to an elevated status in society, and defiantly revelled in the visual excitement and visceral energy of the popular culture emanating from the United States.

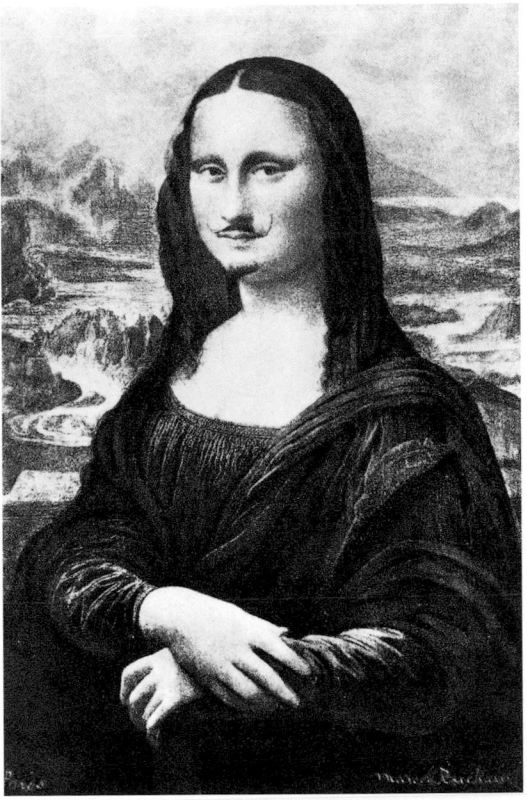

Fig. 1
MARCEL DUCHAMP
L.H.O.O.Q.
1919. Postcard and ink,
17.5 x 12 cm. Private
collection

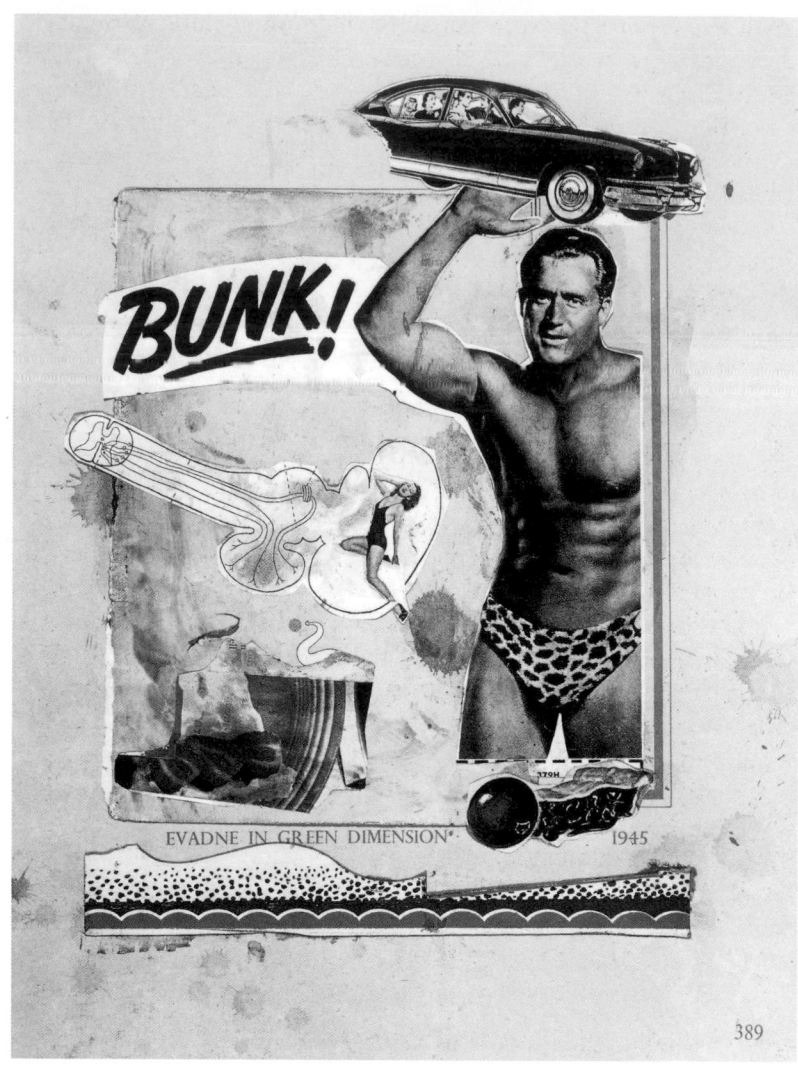

The years immediately following World War II were a gloomy era in Great Britain. The enormous cost of rebuilding after the horrific destruction of the war meant that there was widespread rationing, and any sort of luxury, including colour printing, was looked down upon as frivolous and even unpatriotic. The arts in Britain in the post-war period had an almost defiant drabness. The British films of the period, for example, were nearly all in black and white, and concentrated on the oppressive conditions of life in the lower classes. Clothing was grimly colourless and the architecture bleak and boxy.

The United States, on the other hand, was booming. Untouched by the physical destruction of the war, industry in America was expanding rapidly, and with the growth in wealth there came a technologically advanced popular culture. American magazines and films were big, colourful and glossy, in striking contrast to the essentially monochrome British ethos. For the first time, icons from popular culture seemed to have gained a power in society that rivalled that of politicians and businessmen. It is entirely possible that the two most widely influential Americans in the post-war era were Elvis Presley and Mickey Mouse, both of whom would later become celebrated subjects of paintings by Pop artists such as Andy Warhol (1928–86) and Roy Lichtenstein (1923–).

This desperate grasping for American pop culture horrified idealistic intellectuals such as Herbert Read, who disdained aesthetic pleasure, in the belief that art's mission was to improve. The Independent

Group was the artistic expression of the impulse to embrace the exuberance and the highly finished quality of American popular culture. Paolozzi's collages of the 1940s and 1950s, created independently and in isolation, were the first glimmerings of this rebellion against the dreariness and lofty ideals of the 'official' culture of the post-war era in Britain (see Fig. 2).

The Independent Group's efforts culminated in 1956 in a landmark exhibition at the Whitechapel Art Gallery in London, prophetically called *This Is Tomorrow*. The show incorporated a wide range of images of the sort that would soon become the staples of Pop Art: a blow-up of Marilyn Monroe in *The Seven-Year Itch*; a robot called Robby, which had appeared in an American science-fiction film called *The Forbidden Planet*; poster-sized images of beer bottles and spaghetti. An American jukebox was installed in the gallery, which played the latest hit pop records. The poster for the exhibition was a small collage by Richard Hamilton called *Just What Is It That Makes Today's Homes So Different, So Appealing?* (Plate 7). Neatly combining images of Hollywood film, the comic book, commercial products and exaggerated sexuality, this insouciant send-up of middle-class American culture has been called the first work of Pop Art: the grotesquely over-muscled man who dominates the composition holds in his hand a piece of candy with the word 'POP' emblazoned across it. Hamilton also proved to be an eloquent theorist for the emerging movement. In 1961 he wrote this succinct synopsis of Pop Art's rationale:

> It is the Playboy 'Playmate of the Month' pull-out pin-up which provides us with the closest contemporary equivalent of the odalisque in painting. Automobile body stylists have absorbed the symbolism of the space age more successfully than any artist. Social comment is left to comic strip and TV. Epic has become synonymous with a certain kind of film and the heroic archetype is now buried deep in movie lore. If the artist is not to lose much of his ancient purpose he may have to plunder the popular arts to recover the imagery which is his rightful inheritance.

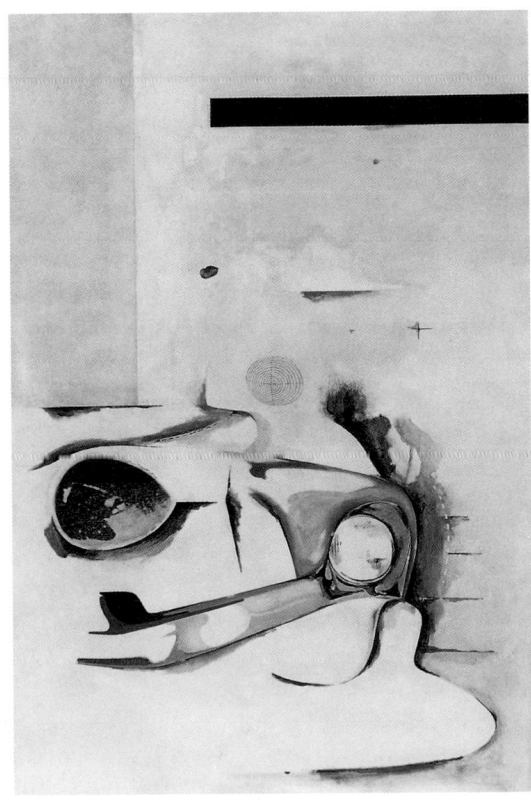

Fig. 3
RICHARD HAMILTON
Hommage à Chrysler Corp
1957. Oil, metal foil and collage on panel, 121.9 x 81 cm. Private collection

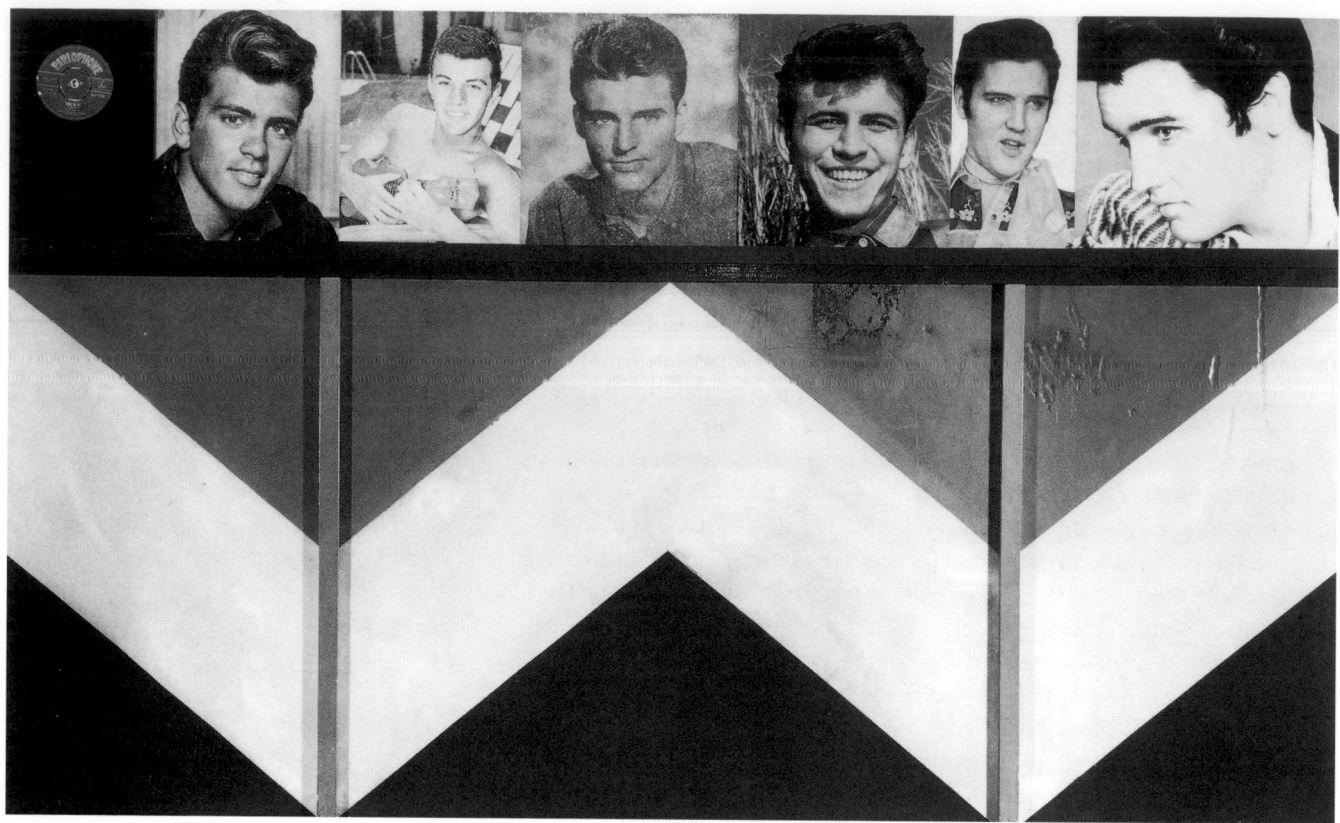

Fig. 4
PETER BLAKE
Got a Girl
1960–1. Enamel,
photo collage and record,
94 x 154.9 x 4.2 cm.
Whitworth Art Gallery,
University of Manchester

After Hamilton had given the movement an image and (according to some versions) Lawrence Alloway had chosen its name, Pop Art began appearing everywhere. Working independently, a young Kentish artist named Peter Blake (1932–) was already producing paintings and collages based upon images from the American-influenced youth culture. In his paintings and in collages utilizing pin-ups of American rock-and-roll singers such as *Got a Girl* (Fig. 4), he appeared to be as much a fan, a part of the popular culture himself, as an artist. In 1967 Blake created one of the most enduring icons of popular culture, the cover of the enormously influential Beatles album *Sgt Pepper's Lonely Hearts Club Band*. Three years later, Andy Warhol would begin producing silkscreened images of movie stars and pop singers, albeit with no trace of Blake's apparent innocence and enthusiasm for his subjects.

At roughly the same time as the Independent Group and Peter Blake were gleefully plundering its popular culture, America, the fecund spawning ground of the imagery, was producing its own strain of Pop Art. Jasper Johns (1930–) began painting canvases of the American flag (Plate 3) and dart targets within months of the appearance of Hamilton's *Just What Is It....* When Johns's paintings were exhibited for the first time, at Leo Castelli's gallery in New York in January 1958, they made an enormous impact. The American art scene at that time was strongly dominated by Abstract Expressionism, which was about as serious and high-minded a school of art as ever existed outside the medieval cloister. Indeed, many of its exponents, such as Jackson Pollock (1912–56), Willem de Kooning (1904–) and Mark Rothko (1903–70), had a deeply spiritual intent in their art. The movement rejected images of the external world as being unnecessarily confining, and sought rather to unleash the artist's inner creative force through the use of spontaneous gesture and a visceral, instinctual approach to colour. Like Surrealism, Abstract Expressionism placed a strong emphasis on the life of the mind, though with none of the

Surrealists' playful sense of irony: the inner life of the artist, and even psychiatric insights into his mental sufferings, were often the 'subject-matter' of the abstract paintings.

In diametrical contrast, one of Jasper Johns's most famous works was actually based upon a joke. As he explained to an interviewer: 'Somebody told me that Bill de Kooning said [of art dealer Leo Castelli] that you could give that son of a bitch two beer cans and he could sell them. I thought, what a wonderful idea for a sculpture.' The work that resulted, *Painted Bronze II: Ale Cans* (Fig. 5), was to be a major influence upon the Pop artists of the 1960s, who frequently turned to commercial design for inspiration. Another of Johns's early sculptures is even more profane. A bronzed pair of shoes with tiny mirrors on the toes, it is an esoteric reference to a practice of American high-school boys in the 1950s and acts as a surreptitious contrivance to enable them to peep up girls' skirts.

Robert Rauschenberg (1925–), the other towering talent of this transitional period in American painting, invented a new medium he called the 'combine painting'. The results are heavily painted abstract compositions that incorporate collage elements such as newspaper clippings in the Cubist tradition, as well as three-dimensional objects, many of them quite large. Most of these objects, seen outside their art context, would have been taken for rubbish: chair backs, broken clocks, Coca-Cola bottles, stuffed birds, old shoes. Rauschenberg's combine paintings, which he first began producing in 1955 (a year before *This Is Tomorrow*), took Duchamp's absurdist utilization of

Fig. 5
JASPER JOHNS
Painted Bronze II:
Ale Cans
1964. Painted bronze, 14 x
20.3 x 11.4 cm. Collection
of the artist

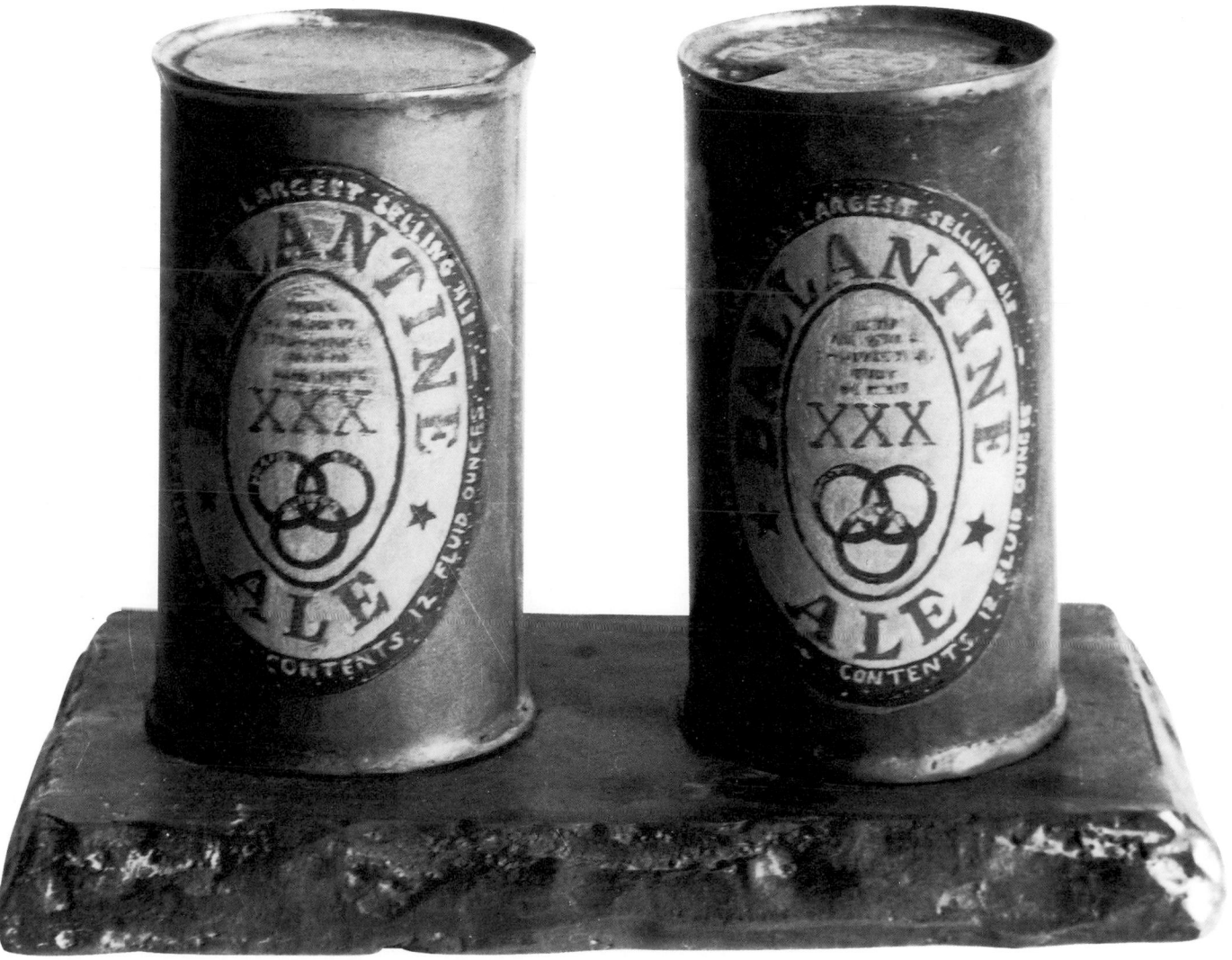

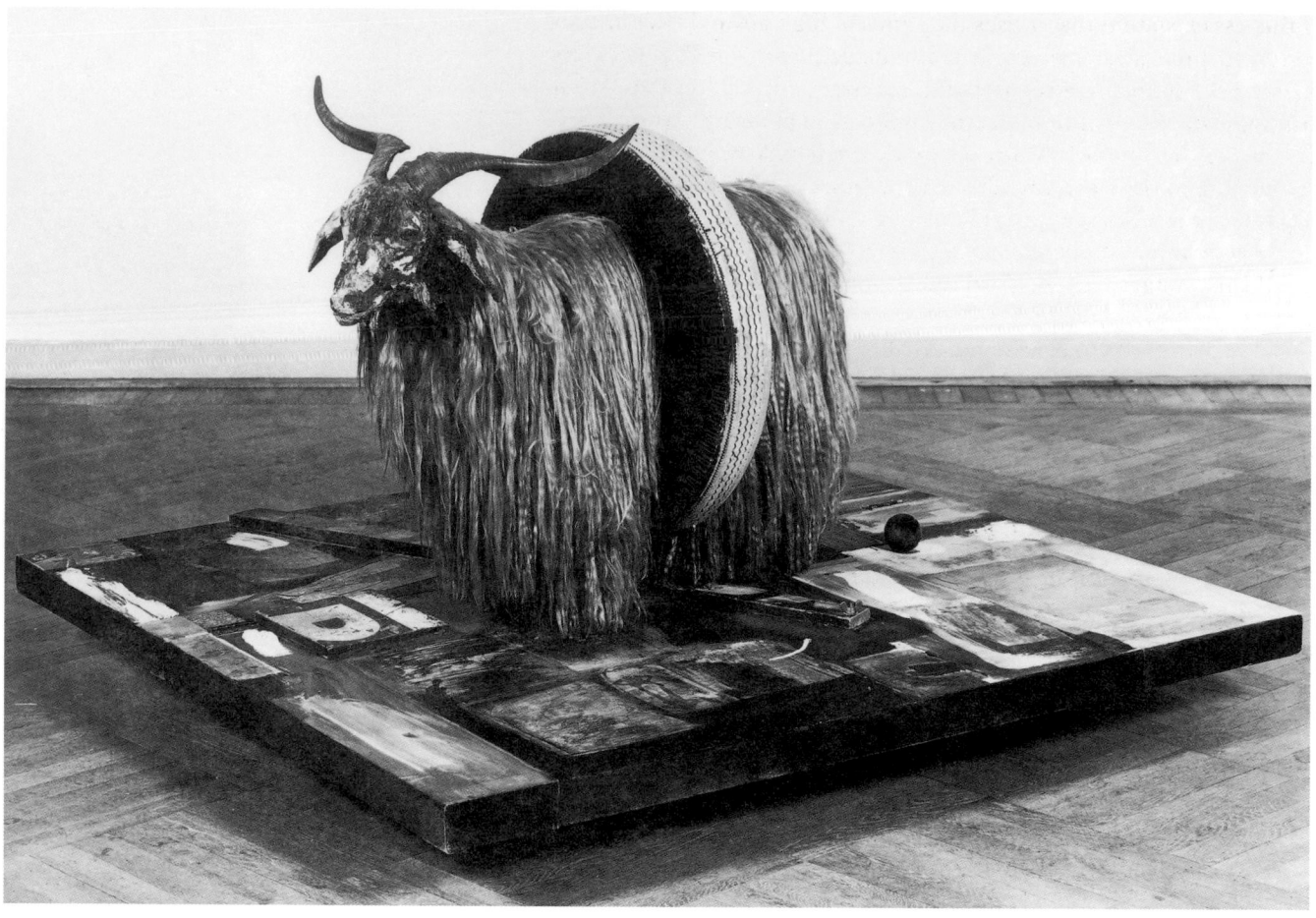

Fig. 6
ROBERT
RAUSCHENBERG
Monogram
1955–9. Stuffed goat, tyre,
wood, canvas, paper and oil
paint, 122.1 x 183 x 183 cm.
Moderna Museet,
Stockholm

everyday objects a step further: things were not simply transformed into art by the artist's fiat, they were actually covered with 'art marks', brushstrokes of oil paint that mimicked the gestures of the Abstract Expressionists. Rauschenberg's most shocking combine painting was called *Bed* (Plate 4): he poured paint over his bedclothes and pillow and hung them on the wall.

While the Independent Group in Britain and Johns and Rauschenberg in the United States incorporated images from everyday life in their work, they were still governed by the traditional notion of art as self-expression. The collages of Paolozzi and Hamilton had a clearly defined satirical intention, and the paintings of the Americans, however unconventional their imagery, still bore the expressive mark of the creator's hand. In 1960, the first paintings in what was to become the classic Pop Art style began to emerge in New York. In that year Andy Warhol produced paintings of the comic-strip characters Dick Tracy and Superman, a tin of peaches and a Coca-Cola bottle. Simultaneously, James Rosenquist (1933–), an artist who supported himself by day as a billboard painter, abruptly abandoned the Abstract Expressionist style he had followed in his fine art and painted a five-metre-long canvas in the style of his billboards; called *President Elect* (Plate 12), it juxtaposes images of the newly elected American president, John F. Kennedy, part of a car and a slice of cake, in bold graphic style. The following year Roy Lichtenstein produced the first of his canvases based upon comic strips, a painting of Mickey Mouse and Donald Duck. Although these early works in the classic Pop style still carried traces of Abstract Expressionism, with drips and brush-marks clearly revealing the artist's hand, a fundamentally different attitude towards the role of the artist was beginning to manifest itself.

The dictionary definition of Pop Art paraphrased at the beginning of this essay, stating that it uses the forms of high art to depict images borrowed from mass culture, is really inadequate. For Pop not only rejected the subject-matter of traditional art: it scorned its ethos. What distinguished Pop Art from previous schools of painting was its rejection of the very notion of artistic style, an attitude it inherited from Dada. Rosenquist's paintings, for example, were produced in the flat, uniform style of commercial billboards, and Lichtenstein, too, soon abandoned the last vestiges of painterly expression, and produced uninflected images taken from comic books and other 'low-brow' sources.

In 1962 Andy Warhol produced his first paintings with silkscreens, the technique which would dominate the rest of his career as a painter. He clipped photographs from newspapers – images of car crashes, baseball games and film stars – and had commercial silkscreens of them prepared. Then he screened the images directly onto canvases, thereby completely eliminating any direct human touch. Millet and Daumier, Stubbs and Wright of Derby had used scenes from everyday life in part because they provided a neutral context in which they might explore traditional painterly issues, such as light and shade, or modelling three-dimensional objects. Moreover, they sometimes used these subjects for a very direct form of expression: to make a political statement. The Pop artists, on the other hand, chose images precisely because they were banal. Warhol, the Wildean epigrammatist of the movement, once commented, with his usual, deliberate vulgarity: 'When you read Genet you get all hot, and that makes some people say this is not art. The thing I like about it is that it makes you forget about style and that sort of thing. Style isn't really important.'

Fig. 7
JAMES ROSENQUIST
The Light That
Won't Fail I
1961. Oil on canvas, 182.1
x 244.3 cm. Hirshhorn
Museum, Smithsonian
Institution, Washington
DC

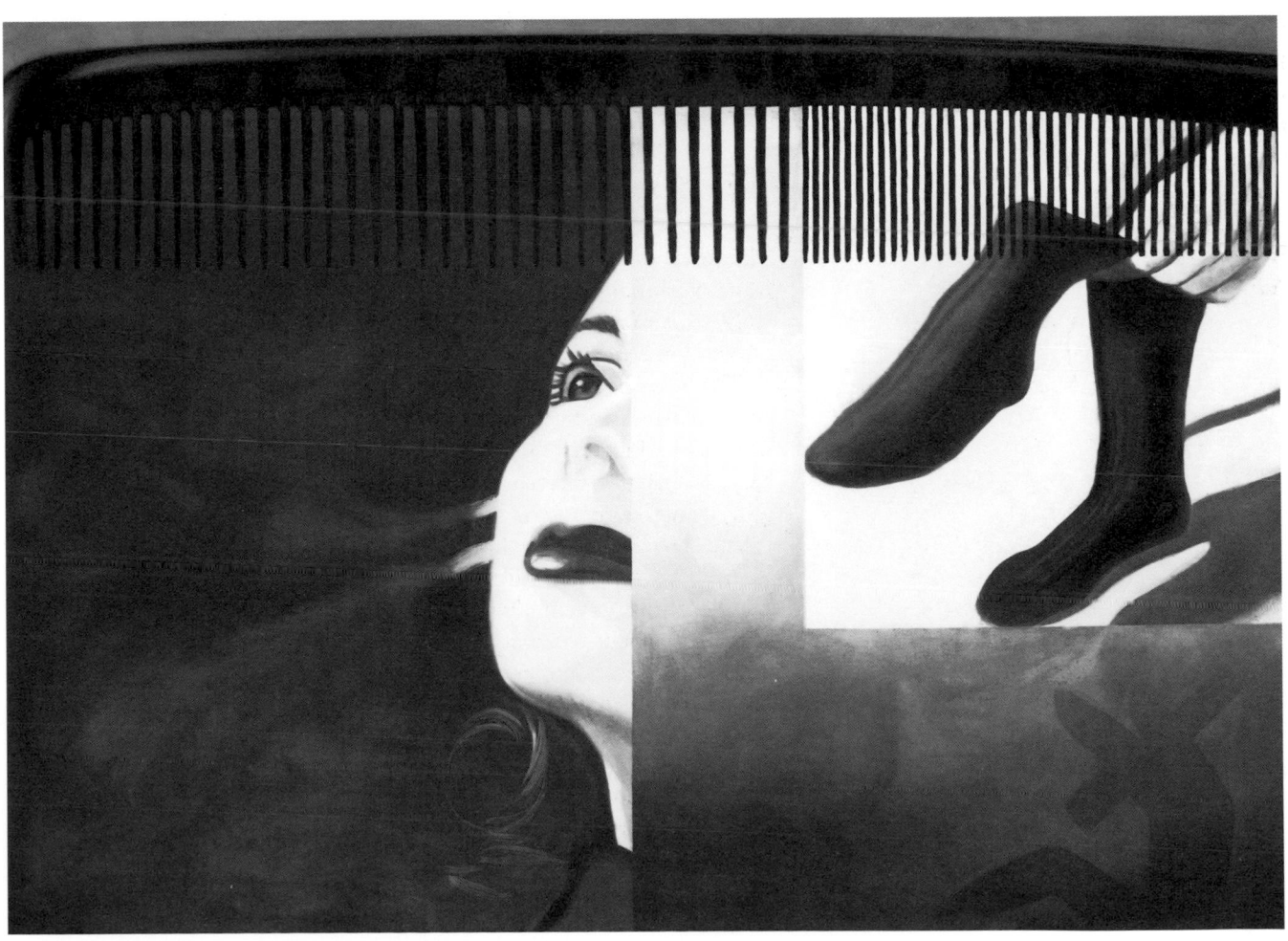

The defining element of American Pop Art of the classic period, implicit in its rejection of style, was something called cool. The word, which comes from the vocabulary of jazz, means that the artist has an attitude of detachment from his work, maintaining an appearance of unconcern or even a lack of interest in what he is doing. For a jazz musician, cool takes the form of a stony face and a low-key manner as he blows a mournful, heart-rending blues. In Pop Art, the cool attitude of detachment is exemplified by the random jumbling together of unrelated images in James Rosenquist's work. In *The Light That Won't Fail I* (Fig. 7), the point of juxtaposing the girl's upturned face with a comb and a pair of socks is not to belittle the subjects. It is rather a cool statement by the artist that all subject-matter interests him equally – which is to say that it does not interest him a great deal. Just as the commercial billboard painter might, in the course of a single week, be asked to paint a bottle of whisky or a carton of milk, a young boy in a pair of blue jeans or a woman in an elegant gown, all rendered in the same flat, depersonalized style, so the Pop artist can combine any miscellaneous assortment of images. The process might be compared with Duchamp's early assemblages, such as *Bicycle Wheel* (Fig. 8). Duchamp mounted a bicycle wheel on the seat of a stool, an absurd combination which resulted in a new object that bluntly affirmed Wilde's aesthetic dictum, 'All art is quite useless'. In much the same way, Rosenquist's billboard-style paintings were cool versions of the narrative murals which had been an essential part of Western art since the time of Giotto (1267–1337); but whereas the medieval and Renaissance world-view was defined by narratives such as the life of Christ and the lives of the saints, by the middle of the twentieth century the life of Everyman was defined by commercial products and celebrities.

With Lichtenstein's comic-strip paintings, it might seem harder to defend the view that the artist is not making a satirical commentary: surely a painting such as *We Rose Up Slowly...* (Fig. 9) must have been intended to be taken ironically, as 'camp'. That is undeniably true, but to leave it at that is to miss the essence of Lichtenstein's art. Obviously, the caricature of physical beauty in his cartoon blondes and their square-jawed boyfriends is ironic. The collectors and gallerygoers who saw these paintings realized the shallowness and absurdity of such a portrayal of romance, whereas the young girls for whom the original comic books were intended did not. It is almost a textbook definition of irony.

Yet what Lichtenstein was really doing in his comic-strip paintings was an exercise in artistic cool. If *We Rose Up Slowly...* has a message, it is that the flat, shallow vision of love in romance comics is as valid as any other vision of love. 'Love', as a subject, has been subordinated to the painter's desire for a bold and striking design. In addition to his romance paintings, Lichtenstein in this early period also painted a large number of paintings based upon war and action comic books. These brilliantly coloured canvases, pulsating with powerful visual excitement (see Plate 24), have the same cool detachment from their real-life subject, war, as the romance-comic paintings do from love.

By addressing love and war, the two great themes of epic poetry, Lichtenstein fulfilled Richard Hamilton's mandate, to recover the eternal themes of Western art from popular culture. Lichtenstein rejected style by making it his subject-matter: it is the precise rendering of the generic comic-book style that gives his early work its impact. And in a sense, conversely, he also made subject-matter his style: for in 1961 it was outrageous for a serious artist to use such banal imagery. The cooler and more restrained his presentation, the more

Fig. 8
MARCEL DUCHAMP
Bicycle Wheel
1913. Original lost; sixth version. Wood and metal, 125.7 x 62.9 cm. Indiana University Art Museum, Bloomington

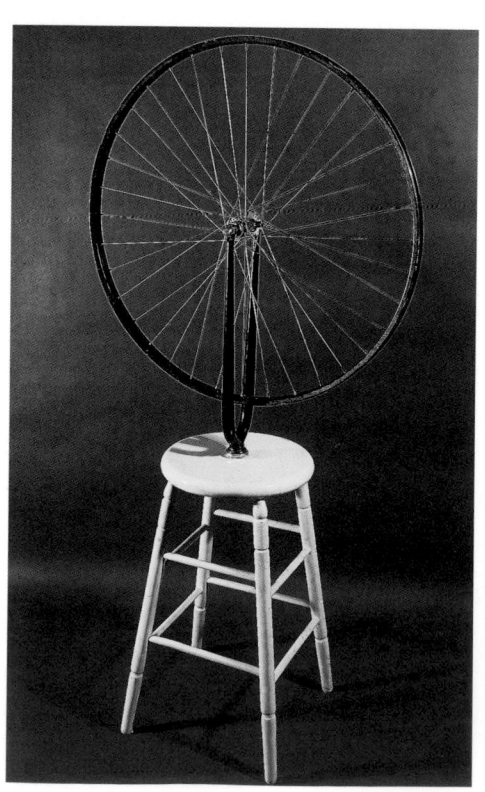

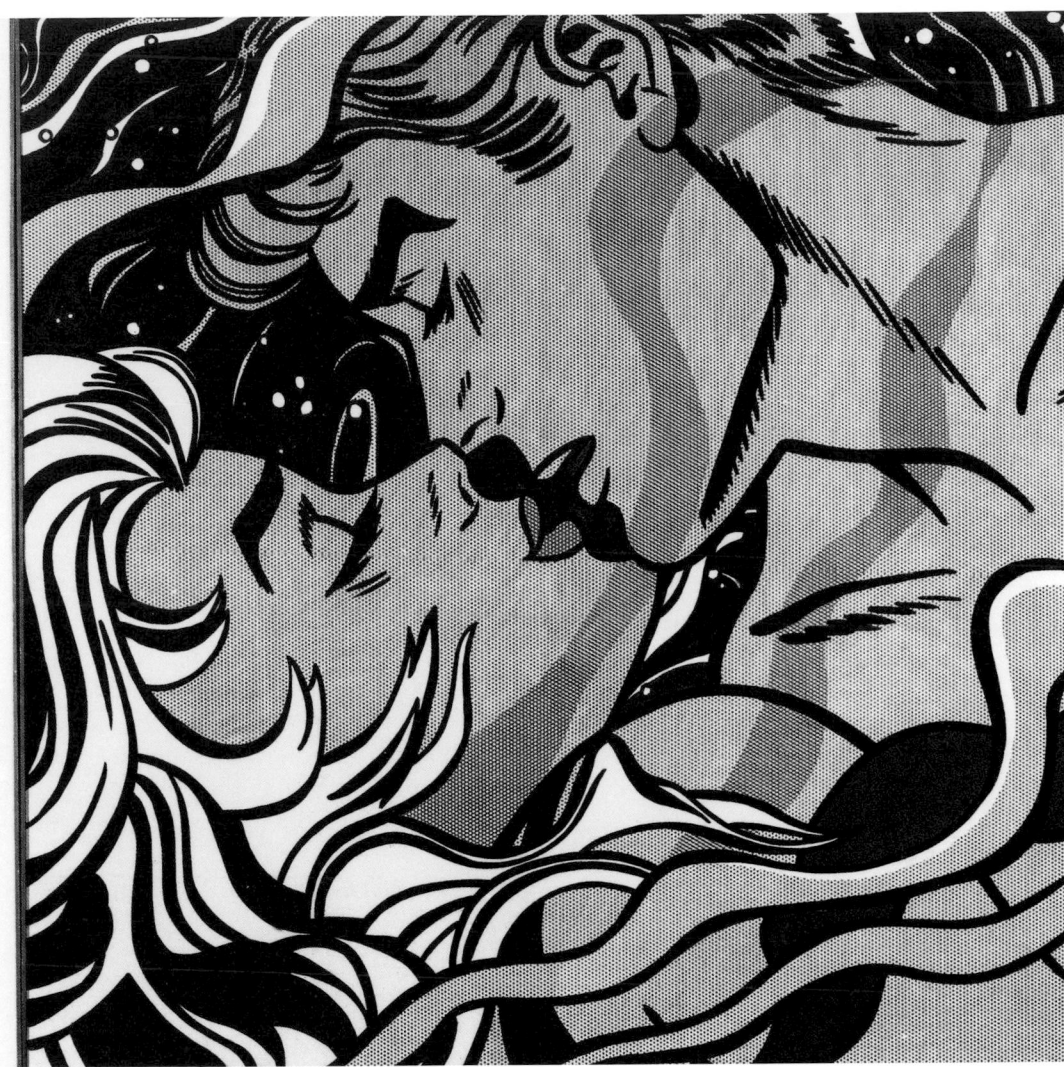

WE ROSE UP SLOWLY ...AS IF WE DIDN'T BELONG TO THE OUTSIDE WORLD ANY LONGER ...LIKE SWIMMERS IN A SHADOWY DREAM ... WHO DIDN'T NEED TO BREATHE...

Fig. 9
ROY LICHTENSTEIN
We Rose Up Slowly
1964. Oil and magna on
canvas, two panels, 172.7 x
61 cm and 172.7 x 172.7
cm. Museum für Moderne
Kunst, Frankfurt

outrageous it seemed. Lichtenstein appeared to reject the basic principle of art as an elevated and enlightening activity. In an interview with the French critic Alain Robbe-Grillet, published in 1968, Lichtenstein said, in the interviewer's paraphrase: 'I have the feeling that these flat images conform far more to what goes inside our heads, than those false depths [of lyrical abstraction or abstract expressionism].' The Pop painters proclaimed an almost defiant identification of themselves with traditional American culture. American artists before them, perhaps as a result of the nation's immigrant heritage, had frequently harboured the belief that in order to be validated as artists they must succeed in Europe. Many of the best American artists, such as Mary Cassatt (1844–1926), James McNeill Whistler (1834–1903) and John Singer Sargent (1856–1925), had spent much or most of their careers in Paris and London. The Pop artists, however, were born in an era when American pop culture, epitomized by the fabulous success of Hollywood, was enjoying a complete, global triumph, and all the world, it seemed, sought to emulate the American example – which was exactly why the British Pop artists' embrace of it constituted such a thumb in the eye of 'official' British culture.

The concept of embracing the mundane, of celebrating the life of the ordinary person, is a theme of American culture going back at least to the poetry of Walt Whitman, the fountainhead of so much American art. Earlier in the twentieth century, the American precisionists, such

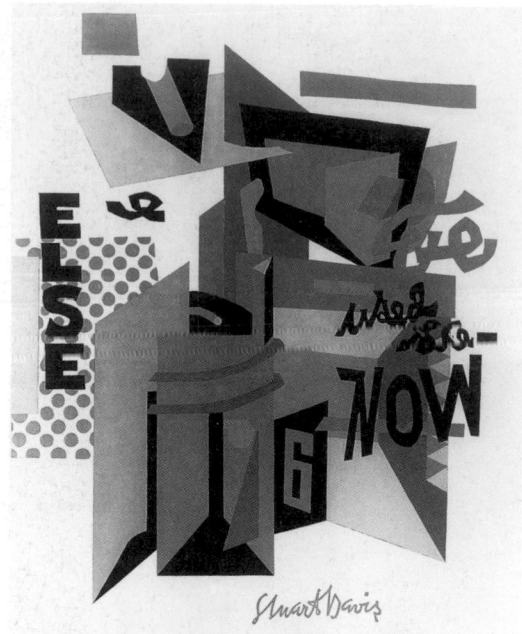

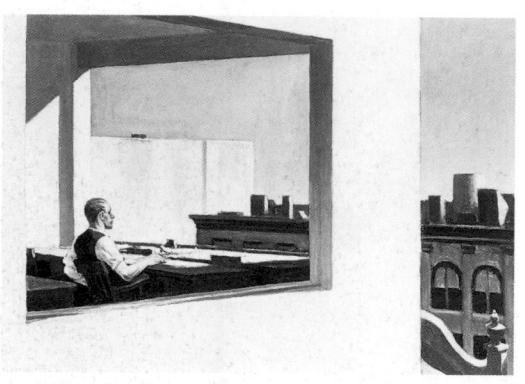

Fig. 10
STUART DAVIS
Owh! In Sao Pao
1951. Oil on canvas, 132.7
x 106 cm. Whitney
Museum of American Art,
New York

Fig. 11
EDWARD HOPPER
Office in a Small City
1953. Oil on canvas, 71.1 x
101.6 cm. Metropolitan
Museum of Art, New York

Fig. 12
ANDY WARHOL
Black and White
Disaster
1963. Acrylic and
silkscreen on canvas,
243.8 x 182.8 cm. Los
Angeles County Museum
of Art, Los Angeles

as Charles Demuth (1883–1935), Georgia O'Keeffe (1887–1986) and Charles Sheeler (1883–1965), had painted urban skylines and industrial scenes, imbuing them with an optimistic, almost mythic glow. The paintings of Stuart Davis (1894–1964) (see Fig. 10) attempted to capture the pulsating energy of New York's streets and boogey-woogey music, even incorporating elements of advertising design. Edward Hopper's (1882–1967) melancholy paintings of lonely people and deserted urban settings (see Fig. 11) also extolled the lives of ordinary people. Of the Pop artists, Rosenquist is closest in spirit to this democratic strain of American art. His *F-111* (Private collection), a vast painting (26 metres in length), combines images of food and machinery in an heroic, promiscuous style that might justly be likened to Whitman's catalogic method: the viewer comes away with the sensation that there is room for all America in a painting so vast. The key difference between the Pop artists and their predecessors is that, despite their deliberate embracing of the crudity and energy of the ordinary, they always maintained an aloof attitude towards their subjects.

Of all the Pop artists, Andy Warhol was perhaps the most profoundly 'American'. Most of the subjects of his paintings from the early 1960s were immediately identifiable as being American: dollar bills, Coca-Cola bottles, Campbell's soup cans (Plate 21), Elvis Presley, Marilyn Monroe (Plate 34), Elizabeth Taylor, Jacqueline Kennedy. At the same time as he was painting images of famous people and commercial products, he was also working on a parallel group of pictures, which was no less American: the Disaster series. Using the silkscreen technique, he made paintings using serial compositions of car crashes, or scenes from a race riot, a suicide leap, the electric chair, firemen performing a rescue (Fig. 12).

While these paintings are obviously a reflection of a troubled era in the United States, it would be a mistake to ascribe a motive of social commentary *per se* to the Disaster paintings. The artist once told an interviewer:

> I think of myself as an American artist. I like it here, I think it's so great. It's fantastic. ... I feel I represent the U.S. in my art, but I'm not a social critic. I just paint those objects in my paintings because those are the things I know best. I'm not trying to criticize the U.S. in any way, not trying to show up any ugliness at all. I'm just a pure artist, I guess.

Andy Warhol was the apotheosis of cool. His mechanistic approach to painting – he once said, 'I think everybody should be a machine', and called his studio the Factory – interposed the greatest possible conceptual gulf between the artist and his work, and therefore between the artist and those who viewed his work. Warhol often said that anyone could paint his paintings as well as he did – and apparently they did. When he revealed that some of his paintings had actually been executed by his assistants, Gerard Malanga and Brigid Polk, he created a small panic in the art market. He immediately retracted the statement, though it was never clear which was factual, the original statement or the retraction. A series of silkscreens of Marilyn Monroe printed in 1967 (Plate 34) were supervised by a printer named David Whitney, and Warhol himself was not even present when the proofs were pulled.

Warhol was probably the most famous artist America has yet produced. His pale, impassive face, topped with a great shock of bleached blond hair, was instantly recognizable to millions of people who never went to art galleries or museums. He himself became part of the popular culture which provided the visual bank for his art; a successful

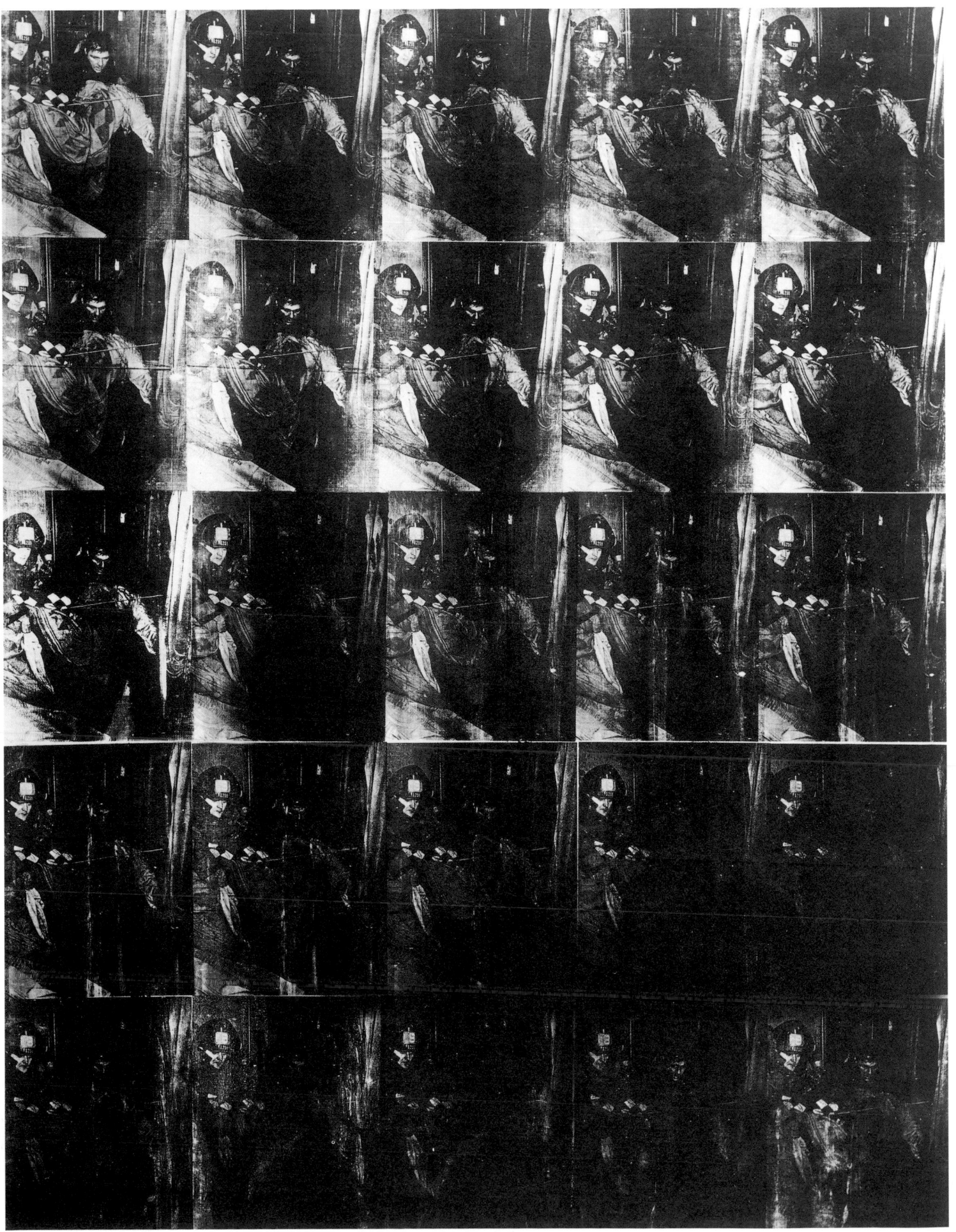

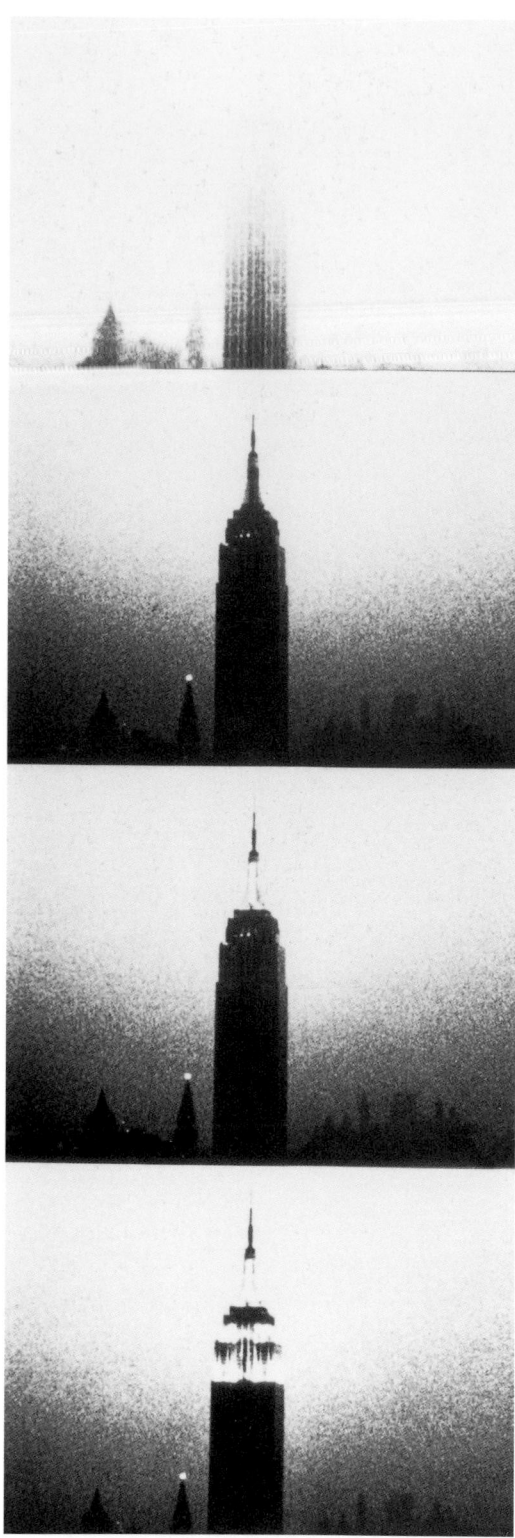

Fig. 13
ANDY WARHOL
Stills from the film
Empire, 1964

commercial artist in the 1950s, even at the peak of his career he was still designing covers for paying customers as diverse as *Time* magazine and the Rolling Stones rock group. In 1963, he turned to the medium which, more than any other, traffics in fame: film. His first efforts were the cinematic equivalent of his silkscreened paintings. He chose a subject – a man sleeping, someone eating a mushroom, a man getting a haircut – and then pointed his camera at it, turned it on and let it run until the film was used up. These films were called, respectively, *Sleep, Eat* and *Haircut*. The most famous of his early films was an eight-hour epic called *Empire* (Fig. 13), a fixed frame film of the Empire State Building shot for nearly six hours, beginning at sundown on 25 July 1964. Warhol never expected that the audience would sit on the edge of their seats, staring at an unchanging (except for the slowly darkening sky) image. Rather, he expected that films such as *Empire* would be the cinematic equivalent of wallpaper (which he later created, for a gallery exhibition in 1966), and he wanted the audience to feel free to talk, eat and do anything they liked as the film rolled inexorably on.

Within two years he was using colour and sound stock to make films that had, if not actual plots, at least dialogue and action. These films, anarchic and formless, frequently with a strong dose of sexual content, were performed by the drifters and hangers-on, many of them transvestites and drug addicts, who frequented the Factory. Joe Dallesandro, who was one of his favourite Superstars, as he called his actors, was discovered when he wandered by mistake into an apartment where Warhol was shooting a film. Sometimes Warhol scripted a very free scenario, sometimes he simply let the 'actors' talk and behave naturally. He himself described his film-making method thus:

> I never liked the idea of picking out certain scenes and pieces of time and putting them together, because then it ends up being different from what really happened – it's just not like life, it seems so corny. What I liked was chunks of time all together, every real moment. ... I only wanted to find great people and let them be themselves and talk about what they usually talked about, and I'd film them for a certain length of time, and that would be the movie.

The most vital phase of Warhol's career came to an abrupt halt on 3 June 1968, when a mentally imbalanced woman named Valerie Solanas walked into the Factory and shot him. Solanas, the founder and sole member of S.C.U.M., the Society for Cutting Up Men, was apparently disgruntled because Warhol, who had used her for small parts in two of his films, had not shown her the attention she thought she deserved. In 1962 Warhol had done a series of paintings based upon tabloid newspaper headlines; the day after he was shot, life imitating art, he himself was the subject of such a headline in the *New York Daily News*.

Another artist who transformed himself into a star was David Hockney (1937–). He was responsible for carrying forward the Pop Art movement in Britain in the early 1960s in a style that was markedly different from that espoused by pioneers such as Paolozzi and Hamilton. It is doubtful whether any British artist of the twentieth century has been the subject of more intensive coverage in the mass media than has Hockney. The parallels with Warhol are striking, beginning with their appearance. When Hockney first arrived in America in 1961 he bleached his hair a loud shade of blond, just as Warhol did. Both men were also homosexual, a fact that had a tremendous influence on Warhol's films (though perhaps little effect on his paintings), and provided Hockney with the subject-matter for many of his most impor-

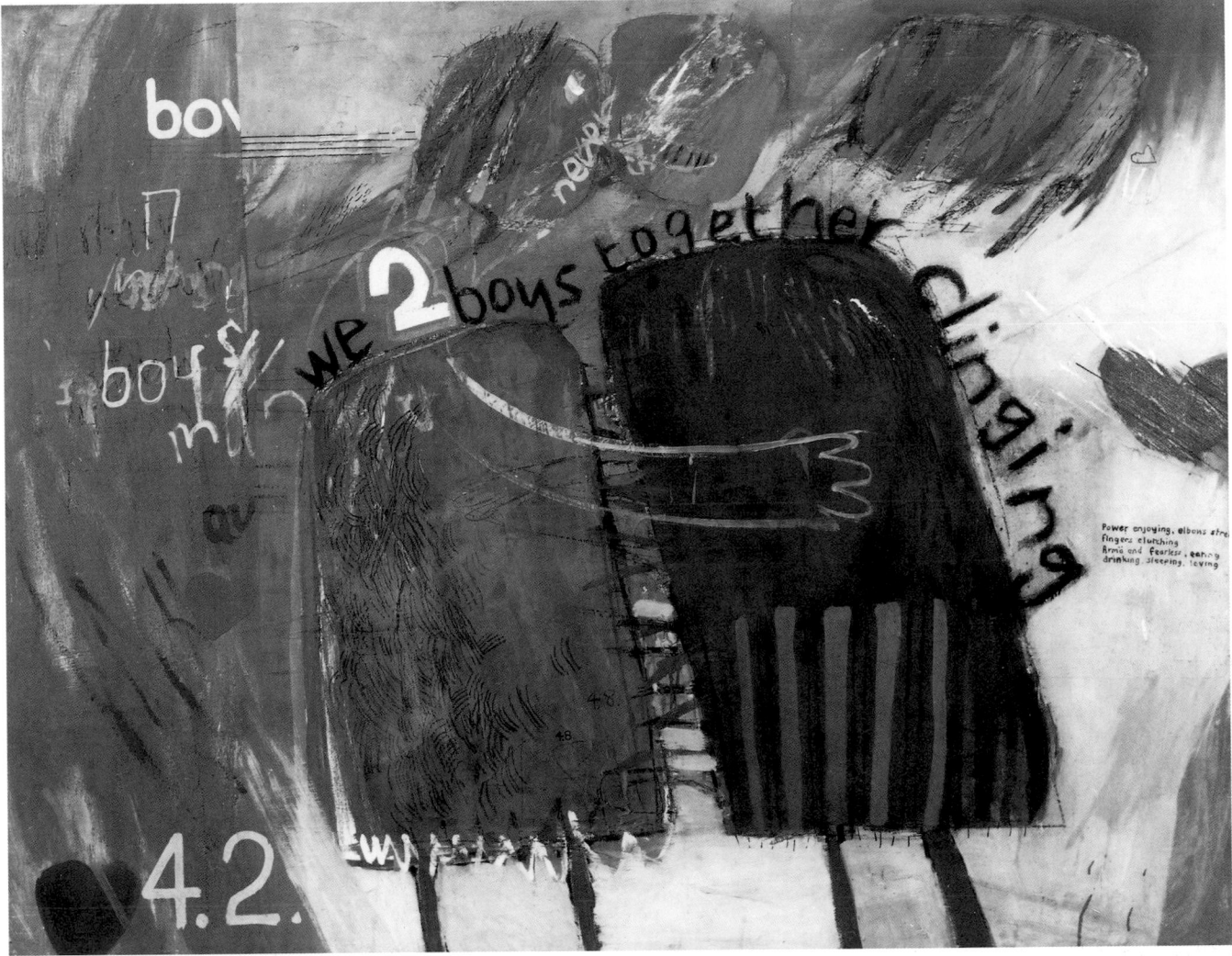

Fig. 14
DAVID HOCKNEY
We Two Boys
Together Clinging
1961. Oil on board, 121.9 x
152.4 cm. Arts Council of
Great Britain, London

tant early works in the Pop mode. While this aspect of Pop Art has frequently been overlooked, in recent years critics and scholars have
examined the issue more forthrightly. In fact, it was widely known in
art circles, but not at all outside them, that Rauschenberg and Johns
were both homosexual, and had been lovers for a period of several
years. Warhol and Hockney were quite open about their sexual identity in an era when it was still taboo, and their careers as artists cannot
be understood fully without taking it into account.

We Two Boys Together Clinging (Fig. 14), painted in a style strongly
influenced by the crude, vigorous *art brut* of Jean Dubuffet (1901–85),
is suffused with a homosexual subtext. The title comes from Walt
Whitman, who was known to have been homosexual, and on the right
side of the canvas, the artist quotes from Whitman's poem, as a rubric
to describe the relationship of the two figures: 'Power enjoying,
elbows stretching, fingers clutching, Arm'd and fearless, eating, drink-
ing, sleeping, loving.' The '4.2.' at the lower left is based on a cipher
system that Hockney borrowed from Whitman. The numerals stand
for the letters D and B, fourth and second in the alphabet, which are
an abbreviation for 'Doll Boy'. That was Hockney's nickname for Cliff
Richard, a handsome British pop star who was very popular at the
time, especially among young British homosexuals. Such covert symbolism, which might be likened to the esoteric symbolism of certain
Renaissance painters, mirrored the clandestine nature of the homosexual community at that time, and contributed toward the artists'
sense that they constituted an outlaw group of sorts.

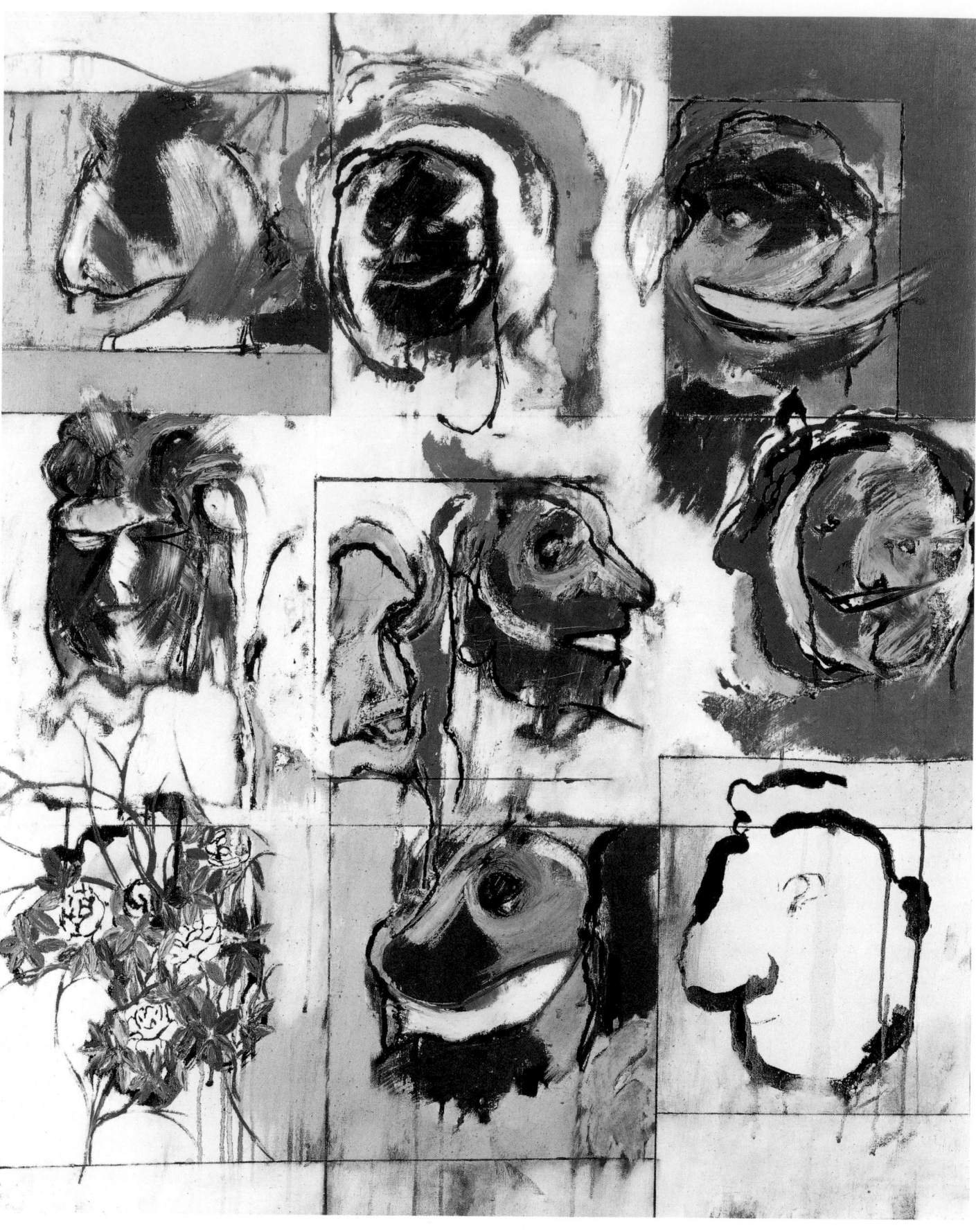

Hockney was the star of his class at the Royal College of Art, which also included Patrick Caulfield (1936–), Peter Phillips (1939–) and the American R.B. Kitaj (1932–). What all these artists shared was a use of graphic techniques in a fine-art context, and a jumbling together of images taken from different sources, so that even entirely painted canvases took on the appearance of a collage. Even as the American Pop artists were moving further away from expressionism of any kind, and disavowing any message in their choice of images, the RCA group was being drawn closer to the modernist mainstream and was either extolling their vulgar sources openly or using them for satirical ends.

Kitaj, by some years the oldest member of the group, functioned in some ways as the mentor of the younger artists, who were dissatisfied with the stodgy didacticism of the Royal Academy. Inspired by Johns and Rauschenberg, he used found imagery in his work, but rather than borrowing from popular culture, in his early works he turned to the literature and high culture of the past. As early as 1958, he based a painting on a series of doodles by the sixteenth-century philosopher Erasmus of Rotterdam (Fig. 15). Doodles by Erasmus hardly qualify as 'low culture', and for this reason Kitaj never fitted entirely comfortably under the Pop label. In his later work, he moved closer to the classic Pop style, even doing a few obligatory comic-strip paintings. Yet even in these works, Kitaj, like Hockney, continued to use graphic techniques borrowed from Abstract Expressionism.

The enormous success of Pop Art in America and Britain in the 1960s inspired imitators throughout the world, and by the end of the decade it had become an international style. It was an art which lent itself readily to being imitated; the methods of the major American Pop artists emphasized reproducibility, and their imagery was deliberately chosen from the most obvious and immediately available sources. The most original and successful Pop artists outside the English-speaking world were both German: Sigmar Polke (1941–) and Gerhard Richter (1932–). Polke's work (see Plate 40) has many affinities with that of Kitaj, notably its frequent use of an esoteric subtext, and it is equally difficult to categorize or even describe. Lisa Leibmann, an American critic, wrote of Polke: 'His body of work encompasses abstraction, figuration, and landscape, has reflected (and affected) a number of concomitant movements in art while remaining exceedingly eccentric, and can variously be described as Pop, political, cryptic, ribald, elegiac, hideous, sumptuous, or just ornery.' Gerhard Richter's early works (see Fig. 25) followed the American models, especially the example of Andy Warhol's Disaster series, very closely. He frequently based his paintings on newspaper photographs, although his works were hand-painted rather than silkscreened. Richter's work, moreover, has none of the cool ambiguity of the American Pop artists, but rather is characterized by a strong political content – much of it, ironically, anti-American in tone.

The most expressionistic of all the Pop artists was the Swedish-born American sculptor Claes Oldenburg (1929–), who created oversized sculptures of commonplace objects that were splashed and dripped with great quantities of colour. In works such as *USA Flag* (Fig. 16), he used some of the painterly effects of the Abstract Expressionists, but with a playful, ironic edge that was altogether alien to them. In 1963 he began to produce soft sculptures, sewing together pieces of cloth and vinyl to produce objects which seemed to be melting. Sculpture, traditionally the most durable of art forms, had reached an insuperable zenith of density and hardness in the 1950s, as seen in the rigid works of artists such as Henry Moore (1898–1986) and Alberto Giacometti (1877–1966). Oldenburg completely rejected this dogma of rigidity in

Fig. 15
R.B. KITAJ
Erasmus Variations
1958. Oil on canvas, 104.2
x 84.2 cm. Private
collection

his soft sculptures, in much the same way that Rosenquist, Lichtenstein and Warhol had renounced the presumed necessity of inner expression in their painting.

Like Warhol, Oldenburg also brought his studio down from the clouds and mingled his art with the life of the streets. In 1961 he rented a storefront at 107 East Twenty-First Street in Manhattan, where he sold sculptural trinkets, small plaster fragments of commercial signs, food and bits of clothing, over the counter, just like any other neighbourhood shop. At the Store, as he called it, Oldenburg and painter Jim Dine (1935–) staged spontaneous multimedia performances, called Happenings (Fig. 22). These anarchic, free-form events, which were somewhere between group art-making and unscripted theatre, had been pioneered two years before by the painter Allen Kaprow (1927–). Oldenburg, despite his Swedish origins (or perhaps because of them) was a fervent believer in the American dream, and openly invoked Walt Whitman as an inspiration. In 1961 he articulated his populist view of art in plainly Whitmanesque style: 'I am for the art of underwear and the art of taxicabs. I am for the art of ice cream cones dropped on concrete. I am for the majestic art of dog-turds, rising like cathedrals.'

While Pop Art was primarily a painters' movement, it did produce some other sculptors of note. George Segal (1924–) created groups of life-sized human figures, made from plaster casts, which he posed in scenes from everyday life, rather like sculptural snapshots. These ambitious works depicted people queuing up at the cinema, buying fuel at the gas station (Plate 27), riding on the bus. Segal's works often incorporated real-life objects as 'props', transporting them to an eerie place pitched halfway between art and reality. Tom Wesselmann (1931–) also combined the human figure, in his case painted, with three-dimensional scenes incorporating real objects, thereby creating a cool version of Rauschenberg's combine paintings. In 'The Great American Nude' series (Plate 29), Wesselmann combined homely interior scenes, which typically included a real wall and articles of furniture, with flat, graphic female nudes in provocatively erotic poses, executed in the cool, uninflected idiom of Rosenquist and Lichtenstein. Marisol (in full, Escobar Marisol) (1930–), an American sculptor born in Paris of Venezuelan parents, carved crude, *faux*-folkish figures in wood and combined them with found objects (Plate 31). Her works often made Pop references, but they are suffused with a gentle satire that sets them apart from the classic Pop style.

The movement's love of the flimsy and its insistent focus on the momentary made it less suitable as an idiom for architecture. Nonetheless, the American architect and critic Robert Venturi was strongly influenced by Pop Art in his scholarly studies of American folk architecture, which celebrated the hot-dog stand, the strip shopping centre, and the pre-fab house. The prevailing International Style of architecture, which was characterized by a strong geometric formalism, had as its motto Mies van der Rohe's dictum, 'Less is more'; Venturi proposed as a response, 'Less is a bore.' In books such as *Complexity and Contradiction in Architecture* and *Learning from Las Vegas*, he advocated an open-minded attitude towards the popular and folk vernacular in public architecture. Many young architects in the 1960s, such as the British firm Archigram, were strongly influenced by Venturi. The group's name, a combination of 'architecture' and 'telegram', proclaimed its intention to restore a sense of urgency and immediacy to a medium which they felt had grown stodgy, stiff and impersonal. Archigram's work is characterized by a strong element of fantasy, which was inspired by American folk architecture. A swimming pool

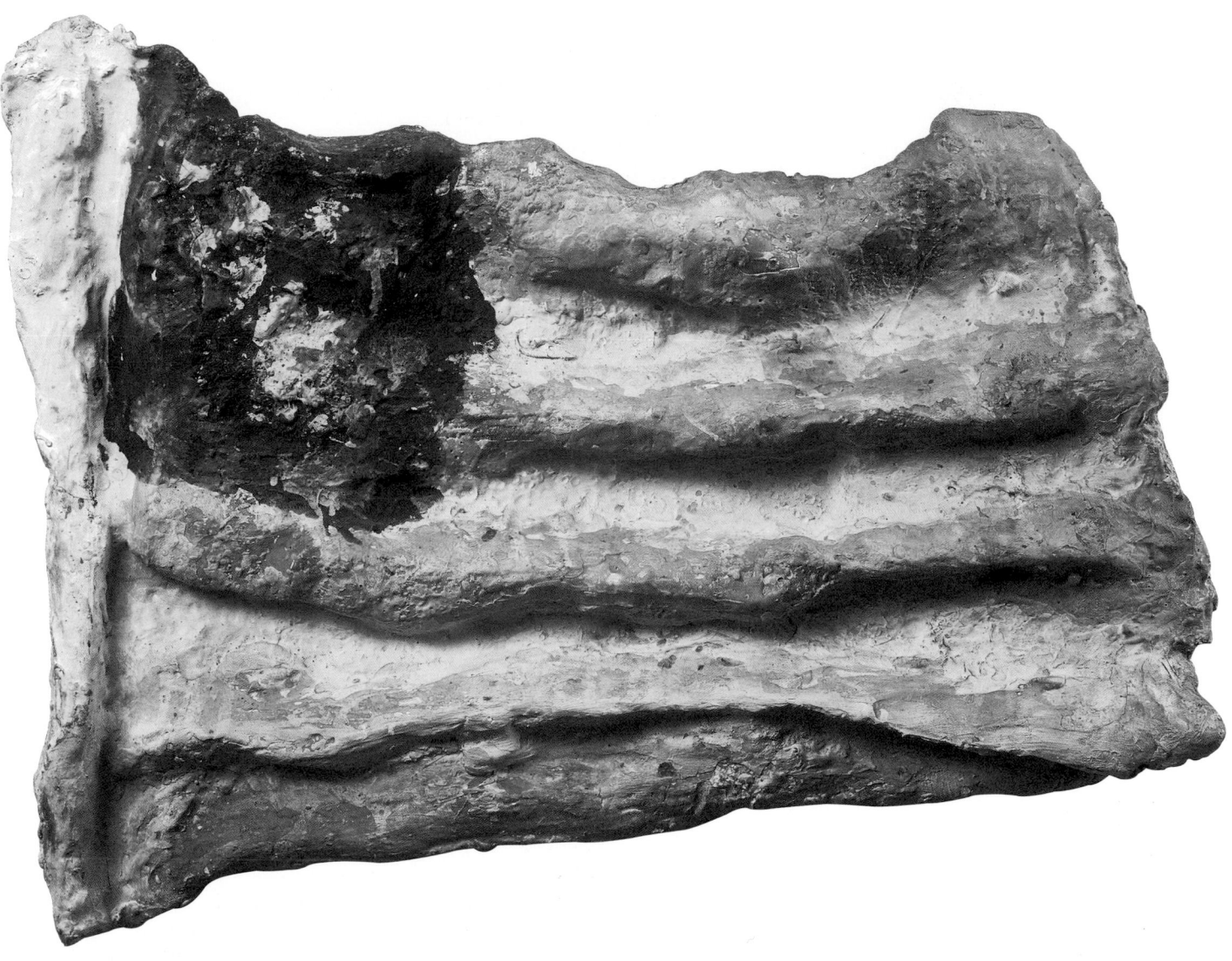

Fig. 16
CLAES OLDENBURG
USA Flag
1960. Muslin soaked in
plaster over wire frame,
painted with tempera, 56.2
x 70.2 x 8.2 cm. Collection
of the artist

they designed for the British rock star Rod Stewart, for example, is shaped in the outline of an electric guitar, a reflection of the luxurious excesses of American pop stars such as Elvis Presley.

While New York and London were simultaneously evolving two distinct schools of Pop Art, yet a third strain was emerging on the American West Coast. As early as 1957, an artist from the state of Kansas named Billy Al Bengston (1934–) was painting canvases of motorcycles and motorcycle parts. He was himself an amateur motorcycle racer of some renown, and his fascination with the technology of the open road pointed the way to a distinctively Californian Pop vision that was as different from the New York school as that of the British artists. Like Rauschenberg and Johns before him, and Hockney after, many of Bengston's paintings have an esoteric meaning; the 'Count Dracula' series (Plate 10), for example, appears to take as its central emblem the silhouette of an iris, but in fact, according to the artist, it represents the moment when the vampire transforms himself from a bat into a man.

Another Midwestern artist who migrated to Los Angeles was Ed Ruscha (1937–). He embraced the Californian way of life even more openly. In some cases his invocations of the American West manage to be at once absolutely forthright and yet mysterious: in *Noise, Pencil, Broken Pencil, Cheap Western* (Private collection), he pasted the cover of a Western magazine onto the canvas, thereby presenting the image of a

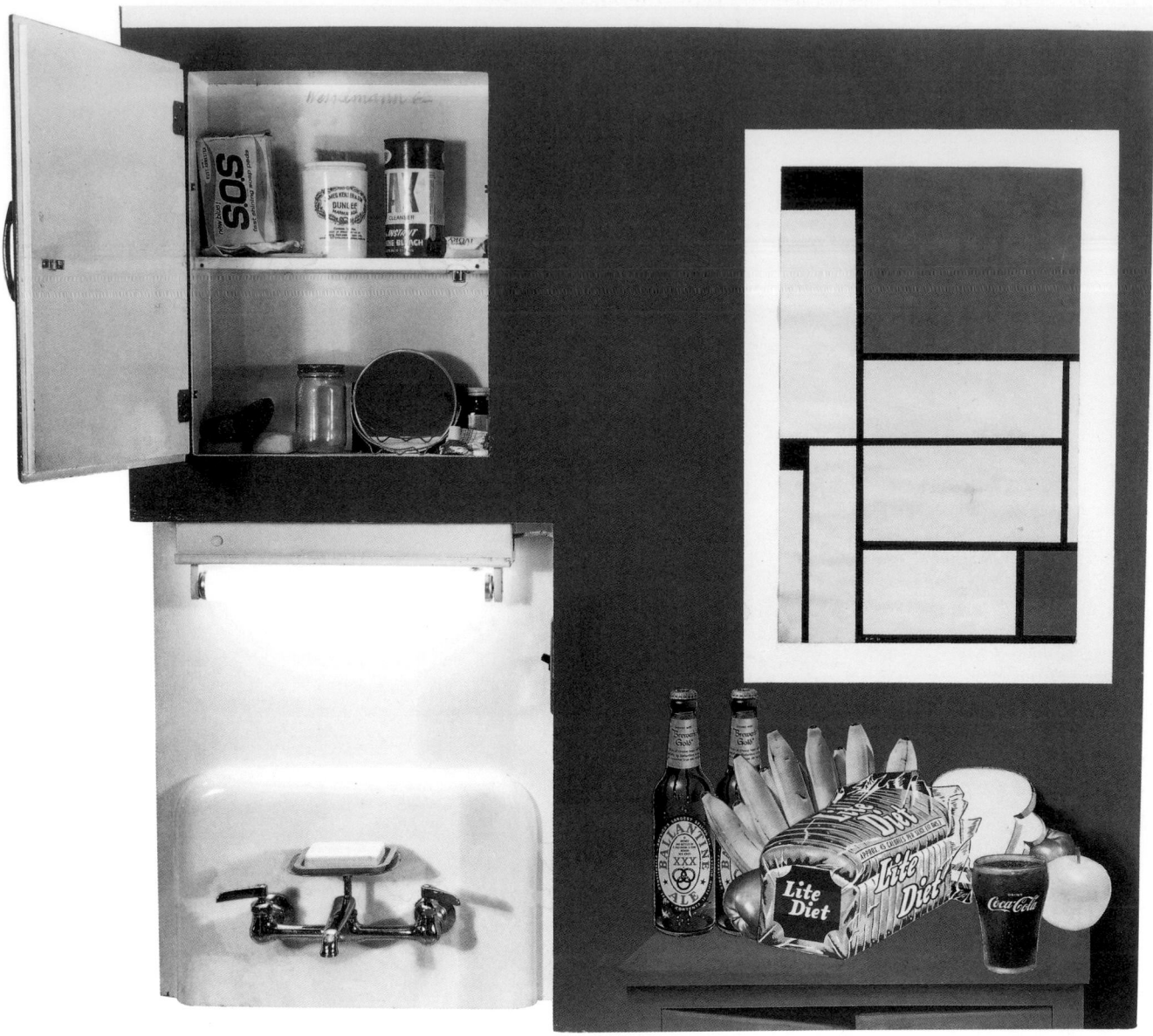

Fig. 17
TOM WESSELMANN
Still Life #20
1962. Collage in paint,
paper, wood, light bulb,
switch, items in chest, etc,
121.9 x 121.9 x 14 cm.
Albright-Knox Art Gallery,
Buffalo, New York

cowboy directly, although the enigmatic context makes the overall effect profoundly ambiguous. Ruscha also produced a great number of boldly designed paintings of words or phrases. *Twentieth Century Fox with Searchlights* (Fig. 24), for example, clearly alludes to the artist's fascination with the image of Southern California as Tinseltown. Ruscha dissected the vapidity and rootlessness of life in California in a series of books, which had titles such as *A Few Palm Trees*, *Thirty-Four Parking Lots in Los Angeles* and *Twenty-Six Gasoline Stations*. They consisted of deadpan, insistently dull photographs, apparently taken with a cheap instant camera, which were gathered together without comment (although in *A Few Palm Trees*, the artist does inform the reader that in every photograph the camera faces west).

There were essential differences between the New York and the Californian schools of Pop Art. Whereas many of the New Yorkers were homosexual, and made no secret of the fact, the West Coast Pop artists projected a macho, tough-guy attitude that was closer to the highly individualistic, hard-drinking and womanizing ethos of the Abstract Expressionists; artists from the two coasts were rarely comfortable in each other's company. Yet there was certainly a stylistic overlap. *Twentieth Century Fox with Searchlights*, for instance, declared a spiritual kinship with the graphic designs of the New York Pop artists.

Lichtenstein, for one, briefly experimented with paintings of single words, as in a canvas from 1962 which boldly proclaimed the word 'ART'.

Many of the Californian artists were painting in an expressive mode that was actually closer, in some ways, to the style of the British Pop artists. Wayne Thiebaud (1920–), a painter based in San Francisco, painted luscious, creamy canvases of bake-shops and dessert trays (Plate 8) that were closer to the early work of R.B. Kitaj than to the Pop style that was then emerging in New York. Mel Ramos (1935–), another artist from the San Francisco Bay area, produced several paintings of cartoon characters in a painterly manner that was also reminiscent of the London school. In 1961–2, Joe Goode (1937–) executed a series of paintings incorporating milk bottles (Plate 17). The canvases were painted solidly in panels of single colour, in the style of minimalist painters such as Ellsworth Kelly (1923–), and the bottle placed in front of them on the gallery floor. Aside from the formal element of the milk bottle, Goode's work lays no certain claim to being Pop Art, though he was a close associate of other Californian Pop artists. After David Hockney moved to Los Angeles in 1964, he immediately devoted himself to his well-known paintings of palm trees, swimming pools and other symbols of California. Almost overnight he became the premier artist of the region, bringing the eye of an enthusiastic immigrant to the Californian way of life, much as Oldenburg had done in New York.

The 1960s were the apogee of Pop Art. What had begun as an anti-art movement eventually became a huge success with museum curators, collectors and many critics, and by the end of the decade enormous sums were being paid for the works of its major exponents. Nothing, perhaps, is deadlier to an avant-garde movement than to become institutionalized, and by the 1980s there was an appreciable diminution in the energy of Pop Art. Andy Warhol, widely regarded as the movement's foremost painter and certainly its most famous personality, died in 1987, which was a great blow to the New York art world. In the 1980s and 1990s, David Hockney has gravitated more and more towards photography and scenic design, creating bold, colourful sets for opera productions on both sides of the Atlantic. Claes Oldenburg has produced large numbers of public monuments, huge sculptures of baseball bats, electric fans and lipstick for public squares. Roy Lichtenstein has become one of the most successful artists in history, from the financial point of view: by the mid-1990s, his large paintings were selling for as much as two million pounds sterling, before the paint had dried. He, too, was commissioned to paint murals for many public and professional spaces, ranging from the lobbies of corporate headquarters to the walls of the New York subway system.

The foregoing ought not to be construed to mean that these later works do not possess high artistic merit; as with the work of Pop Art's classic phase, there is a great range in quality. The point, rather, is that in their maturity the Pop artists became the Establishment that they had formerly rebelled against, and devoted themselves to reworking themes and motifs from the movement's classic period. The imagery of Pop Art, which had originally seemed revolutionary precisely because it was commonplace, ironically, became commonplace itself. Thirty years after *This Is Tomorrow*, the use of images borrowed from low culture in high art had become virtually a convention in transatlantic art, a staple of student work at art schools throughout America and Great Britain.

Nonetheless, the irreverent attitude of Pop Art has continued to be a very powerful force in the contemporary art scene, and many of the most innovative young artists of the 1970s and 1980s modelled their careers closely on those of the movement's masters. In the decade of the 1980s, the most vital force in painting in New York came from the graffiti artists, young painters living the dangerous life of the outlaw on the edges of society, who illegally painted the surfaces of walls, sidewalks and subway trains. Their art derived directly from the dynamic graphic style of the Pop artists, especially the comic-strip painters. They used ephemeral media such as chalk, or industrial products such as canned spray paint and thick ink markers, to create work that epitomized the populist art of the street advocated by Oldenburg and other Pop artists.

The undisputed master of the genre was Keith Haring (1958–90). Like Warhol, Haring became a household name, a celebrity whose prankish calligraphic style grew to be instantly recognizable throughout the world. His career began in the early 1980s in Manhattan, where he drew his distinctive cartoon figures in chalk and industrial markers on the city's walls and pavements. He also created mock tabloid newspapers; in 1980–1 the streets of Greenwich Village were plastered with posters depicting the front page of the *New York Post* with satirical headlines such as REAGAN SLAIN BY HERO COP and MOB FLEES AT POPE RALLY.

In 1982, Haring began to paint on canvas, using extremely vibrant, fluorescent colours and the markers he had been using in his street art. Most of his work was not Pop Art in the strictest sense, for he did not borrow his images from mass culture; rather, he invented his own emblems and drew them in a simplified, schematic style that resembled that of the comic strips (see Plates 45 and 46). He was discovered by an art dealer named Tony Shafrazi. Shafrazi gained notoriety in 1974 when he defaced Picasso's masterpiece *Guernica*, then at the Museum of Modern Art in New York, by spray painting the words 'Kill Lies All' across its surface, all the while shouting 'I am an artist!'. He first hired Haring as an assistant, and then he represented him with great success. Shafrazi also represented Kenny Scharf (1958–), another graffiti artist who was a classmate of Haring's at art school and a close friend. Scharf's work was much more highly polished, and incorporated images taken directly from mass culture in a phantasmagoric style that was heavily influenced by the psychedelic posters and underground comics of the hippie culture of the 1960s.

By the end of the decade, graffiti art held a position in the New York art scene almost as great as that of Pop Art fifteen years earlier, although the museums were slow to accept its street-scruffy style. Warhol, who was a close friend and collaborator of Haring's (see Fig. 18), presided over his artistic progeny as a sort of elder statesman. After his death, Haring said: 'Whatever I've done would not have been possible without Andy. Had Andy not broken the concept of what art is supposed to be, I just wouldn't have been able to exist.' Haring died of AIDS in 1990, at the age of thirty-one.

Cindy Sherman (1954–), another important artist to emerge in New York in the 1970s, was also profoundly influenced by Pop Art, but in a quite different way. Sherman has shot hundreds of heavily art-directed photographs of herself, in widely different costumes and settings, which she calls film stills. The earliest of these, in black and white, mimic the exaggerated melodrama and sentimentality of the *film noir* Hollywood movies of the 1950s and early 1960s; in her later, colour photographs Sherman has shifted to lurid, grotesque imagery that reflects the cheap thrills of brutal horror movies. Sherman has put her own spin on the formula of Pop Art: rather than taking her images from sources in the popular culture, she has created warped, surrealistic simulacra of those sources.

NEW YORK POST

TODAY
Variably cloudy, 80s

TONIGHT
Fair, humid, low

TOMORROW
Partly sunny, mid 80

Details, Page 2

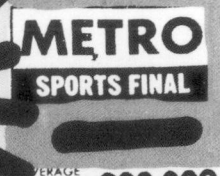

METRO
SPORTS FINAL

AVERAGE
SALES EXCEED **900,000**

MADONNA: 'I'M NOT ASHAMED'

Rock star shrugs off nudie pix furor
STORY PAGE FOUR

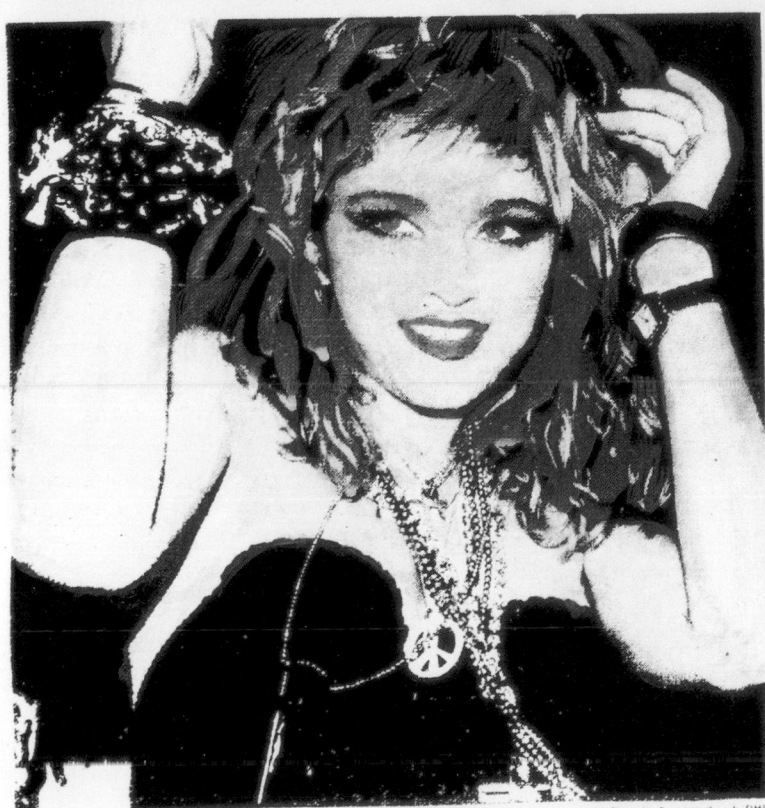

RAUNCHY STAR Madonna in action: No secrets, no shame.

Photo by David McGough, DMI

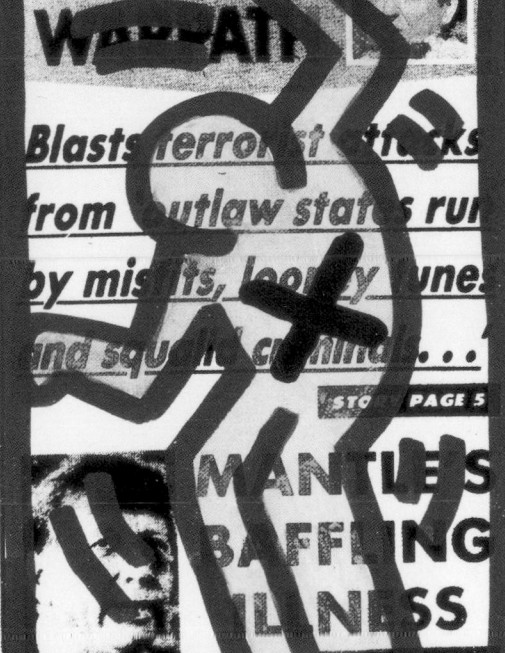

PREZ WRATH

Blasts terrorist attacks from outlaw states run by misfits, loony tunes and squalid criminals...

STORY PAGE 5

MANTLE'S BAFFLING ILLNESS

Perhaps the most outrageous of all the young artists continuing to work in the Pop vein is Jeff Koons (1955–), who reaches to the very lowest depths of banality for his images. Most of his early works consisted of commercial objects absurdly juxtaposed, very much in the spirit of Marcel Duchamp's *Bicycle Wheel* (Fig. 8): basketballs bobbing in an aquarium, a Hoover vacuum cleaner attached to a pair of fluorescent light tubes. In the 1980s he began to make replicas of ugly, tasteless articles of kitsch, such as commercial statuettes of beribboned dogs (Plate 47) and the pop star Michael Jackson. Critic Robert Rosenblum has written of Koons:

> I still recall the shock of my initial confrontation with Koons's lovingly hideous and accurate reconstructions of the lowest levels of three-dimensional kitsch ... head on and up close at its mind-boggling ugliness and deliriously vapid expressions. The bells that finally rang, at least for me, chimed all the way back to 1962, when I first saw Lichtenstein's earliest Pop paintings at Leo Castelli's and stared with disbelief at the colossal gall of an artist who would pollute the space of art with such contemptibly low-brow images.

Of course, not everyone agrees that the 'mind-boggling ugliness and deliriously vapid expressions' of Jeff Koons are a positive contribution to art. Nor, for that matter, has the sexual explicitness of Keith Haring's graffiti art nor the horrific grotesquerie of Cindy Sherman's recent photographs been greeted with open arms in every quarter. The most recent progeny of Pop remain controversial figures, and the notion of ugly art, like that of anti-art before it, will never be universally or even widely acceptable.

Pop Art itself was widely reviled when it was first exhibited, both in Britain and America. There has not been scope here to examine the wide spectrum of critical reaction to the movement, but throughout much of its history, Pop Art has been regarded with great hostility by many critics, dealers and curators. Certainly there have been a great many artists in Britain and America during the time period covered in this book who have continued to work, with great success, within the confines of traditional, art-on-its-pedestal aesthetics. Yet it is nonetheless true to say that no serious artist at the end of the twentieth century can remain entirely immune to the repercussions of Pop Art: art may always be put back on its pedestal, but it will never again rest there quite as securely.

Select Bibliography

Michael Middleton, *Eduardo Paolozzi*, London, 1963

Harold Rosenberg, *The Anxious Object*, New York, 1964

Mario Amaya, *Pop as Art: A Survey of the New Super-Realism*, London and New York, 1965

Michael Kirby, *Happenings*, New York, 1965

John Rublowsky, *Pop Art: Images of the American Dream*, New York, 1965

Allen Kaprow, *Assemblage, Environments and Happenings*, New York, 1966

Lucy Lippard, *Pop Art*, London and New York, 1966

Max Kozloff, *Jasper Johns*, New York, 1967

Claes Oldenburg and Emmett Williams, *Store Days*, New York, 1967

Alan Solomon, *New York: The New Art Scene*, New York, 1967

James Monte, *Billy Al Bengston* (catalogue of an exhibition organized by the Los Angeles County Museum of Art), 1968

Andrew Forge, *Rauschenberg*, New York, 1969

Henry Geldzahler, *New York Painting and Sculpture: 1940–1970*, New York, 1969

John Russell and Suzi Gablik, *Pop Art Redefined*, London and New York, 1969

Michael Compton, *Pop Art*, London, 1970

Rainer Crone, *Andy Warhol*, New York, 1970

Jack Gordon, *Jim Dine*, New York, 1970

Barbara Rose, *Oldenburg*, New York, 1970

John Coplans, *Andy Warhol*, New York, 1971

Marcia Tucker, *James Rosenquist* (catalogue of an exhibition organized by the Whitney Museum of American Art, New York), 1972

Gregory Battcock (ed.), *The New Art: A Critical Anthology*, New York, 1973

Lawrence Alloway, *American Pop Art*, New York and London, 1974

Lawrence Alloway, *Topics in American Art Since 1945*, New York, 1975

Elizabeth Bailey, *Pop Art*, London, 1976

Jose Pierre, *Pop Art: An Illustrated Dictionary*, London, 1977

Irving Sandler, *The New York School: The Painters & Sculptors of the Fifties*, New York, 1978

Andy Warhol and Pat Hackett, *POPism: The Warhol '60s*, New York and London, 1980

Barbara Haskell, *Blam! The Explosion of Pop, Minimalism, and Performance (1958–1964)*, New York and London, 1984

Robert and Mary Pelfrey, *Art and Mass Media*, New York, 1985

Simon Frith, *Art into Pop*, London and New York, 1987

John Walker, *Cross-Overs: Art into Pop, Pop into Art*, New York, 1987

Irving Sandler, *American Art of the 1960s*, New York, 1988

Calvin Tomkins, *Post- to Neo-*, New York, 1988

Maurice Tuchman, and Stephanie Barron, *David Hockney: A Retrospective* (catalogue of an exhibition organized by the Los Angeles County Museum of Art), 1988

Paul Taylor (ed.) *Post-Pop Art*, Cambridge, Massachusetts, 1989

David Robbins (ed.), *The Independent Group: Postwar Britain and the Aesthetics of Plenty* (catalogue of an exhibition organized by the Institute of Contemporary Art, London), 1990

Marco Livingstone, *Pop Art: A Continuing History*, New York and London, 1990

Kirk Varnedoe and Adam Gopnik, *High and Low: Modern Art and Popular Culture* (catalogue of an exhibition organized by the Museum of Modern Art, New York), 1990

John Gruen, *Keith Haring*, New York, 1991

Marco Livingstone (ed.), *Pop Art* (catalogue of an exhibition organized by the Royal Academy of Art, London), 1991

Russell Ferguson (ed.), *Hand-Painted Pop: American Art in Transition 1955–62* (catalogue of an exhibition organized by the Museum of Contemporary Art, Los Angeles), 1992

Diane Waldman, *Roy Lichtenstein* (catalogue of an exhibition organized by the Solomon R. Guggenheim Museum, New York), 1993

List of Illustrations

Colour Plates

1 EDUARDO PAOLOZZI
I Was a Rich Man's Plaything
c1947. Collage, 35.9 x 23.8 cm.
Tate Gallery, London

2 LARRY RIVERS
Washington Crossing the Delaware
1953. Oil on canvas, 210.8 x 281.9 cm. Museum
of Modern Art, New York

3 JASPER JOHNS
Flag
1955. Encaustic, oil and collage on fabric mounted
on plywood, 107.3 x 153.8 cm. Museum of Modern
Art, New York

4 ROBERT RAUSCHENBERG
Bed
1955. Combine painting, 191.1 x 80 x 20.3 cm.
Museum of Modern Art, New York

5 PETER BLAKE
On the Balcony
1955–7. Oil on canvas, 121.3 x 90.8 cm.
Tate Gallery, London

6 ROBERT RAUSCHENBERG
Odalisque
1955–8. Construction, 205.7 x 63.5 x 63.5 cm.
Museum Ludwig, Cologne

7 RICHARD HAMILTON
Just What Is It That Makes Today's Homes
So Different, So Appealing?
1956. Collage, 26 x 25 cm. Kunsthalle, Tübingen

8 WAYNE THIEBAUD
Store Window
1957. Oil on board, 27.9 x 30.5 cm. Private collection

9 JASPER JOHNS
White Numbers
1958. Encaustic on canvas, 170.2 x 125.8 cm.
Museum Ludwig, Cologne

10 BILLY AL BENGSTON
Count Dracula II
1960. Oil on canvas, 121.9 x 121.9 cm.
Newport Harbor Art Museum, Newport Beach

11 R.B. KITAJ
The Murder of Rosa Luxemburg
1960. Oil and collage on canvas, 152.5 x 152.5 cm.
Tate Gallery, London

12 JAMES ROSENQUIST
President Elect
1960–1. Oil on masonite, 226.1 x 505.5 cm.
Musée Nationale d'Art Moderne, Paris

13 PETER BLAKE
Self Portrait with Badges
1961. Oil on hardboard, 172.7 x 120.6 cm.
Tate Gallery, London

14 DAVID HOCKNEY
Tea Painting in an Illusionistic Style
1961. Oil on canvas, 185 x 76 cm. Private collection

15 DAVID HOCKNEY
The Most Beautiful Boy in the World
1961. Oil on canvas, 177.8 x 100.3 cm.
Private collection

16 JAMES ROSENQUIST
I Love You with my Ford
1961. Oil on canvas, 86.4 x 91.4 cm.
Moderna Museet, Stockholm

17 JOE GOODE
Milk Bottle Painting (Two-Part Blue)
1961–2. Oil on canvas with oil on glass bottle,
174 x 167.6 cm. Private collection

18 JIM DINE
Child's Blue Wall
1962. Oil on canvas, wood, metal, light bulb,
152.4 x 182.9 cm. Albright-Knox Art Gallery,
Buffalo, New York

19 JASPER JOHNS
Fool's House
1962. Oil on canvas with objects, 182.9 x 91.4 cm.
Private collection

20 ROY LICHTENSTEIN
George Washington
1962. Oil on canvas, 129.5 x 96.5 cm.
Private collection

21 ANDY WARHOL
Big Campbell's Soup Can (19¢)
1962. Acrylic and graphite on canvas, 182.9
x 138.4 cm. The Menil Collection, Houston

22 PATRICK CAULFIELD
Christ at Emmaus
1963. Oil on board, 101.7 x 127 cm. Royal College
of Art, London

23 ROBERT INDIANA
The X-5
1963. Oil on canvas, 274.3 x 274.3 cm. Whitney
Museum of American Art, New York

24 ROY LICHTENSTEIN
Whaam!
1963. Oil and magna on canvas, 172.7 x 406.4 cm.
Tate Gallery, London

25 CLAES OLDENBURG
Bedroom Ensemble
1963. Wood, vinyl, metal, fake fur, other materials,
518.2 x 640 cm. National Gallery of Canada, Ottawa

26 ED RUSCHA
Noise
1963. Oil on canvas, 183 x 170.2 cm. Private
collection

27 GEORGE SEGAL
The Gas Station
1963. Plaster and mixed media, 259.1 x 731.5 x
121.9 cm. National Gallery of Canada, Ottawa

28 ANDY WARHOL
Red Race Riot
1963. Silkscreen ink on synthetic polymer paint on
canvas, 350 x 210 cm. Museum Ludwig, Cologne

29 TOM WESSELMANN
Bathtub Nude Number 3
1963. Mixed media, 213.4 x 269.2 x 45.1 cm.
Museum Ludwig, Cologne

30 RICHARD HAMILTON
Interior II
1964. Oil, collage, metal relief, cellulose on panel,
121.9 x 162.6 cm. Tate Gallery, London

31 MARISOL
Women and Dog
1964. Mixed media, 182.9 x 208.3 x 40.6 cm.
Whitney Museum of American Art, New York

32 ROBERT RAUSCHENBERG
Persimmon
1964. Oil on canvas with silkscreen, 167.6 x 127 cm.
Private collection

33 JAMES ROSENQUIST
Untitled, Joan Crawford Says
1964. Oil on canvas, 233.7 x 198.1 cm.
Museum Ludwig, Cologne

34 ANDY WARHOL
Marilyn
1967. Serigraph, printed in colour composition,
91.5 x 91.5 cm. Museum of Modern Art, New York

35 EDUARDO PAOLOZZI
Wittgenstein in New York
1965. Screen-print, 96 x 66 cm. Scottish National
Gallery of Modern Art, Edinburgh

36 MEL RAMOS
Micronite Mary
1965. Oil on canvas, 177.8 x 155 cm.
Private collection

37 PETER PHILLIPS
Custom Painting No. 5
1965. Acrylic on canvas, 172 x 300 cm.
Galerie Bischofberger, Zürich

38 CLAES OLDENBURG
Shoestring Potatoes Spilling from a Bag
1965–6. Canvas filled with kapok, painted with glue
and Liquitex, 269.2 x 116.8 x 106.7 cm. Walker Art
Center, Minneapolis

39 ED RUSCHA
The Los Angeles County Museum
of Art on Fire
1965–8. Oil on canvas, 135.9 x 339.1 cm. Hirshhorn
Museum, Smithsonian Institution, Washington DC

Text Illustrations

Comparative Illustrations

1

Eduardo Paolozzi (1924–)
I Was a Rich Man's Plaything

c 1947. Collage, 35.9 x 23.8 cm. Tate Gallery, London

While living in Paris between 1947 and 1949, the Scottish artist Eduardo Paolozzi amassed an enormous collection of visual sources, most of them taken from American newspapers and magazines. He pasted scraps of these images into a notebook, which was never intended for public exhibition but was instead a sort of reference bank, to be drawn on as needed, like a writer's commonplace book. This page from Paolozzi's notebook anticipates Pop Art directly, by incorporating both the word itself (one American critic recently proclaimed that *I Was a Rich Man's Plaything* contained the first appearance of the word 'Pop' in 'a fine art context') and by using images of the sort that would later become staples of the movement. The exaggerated sexuality of the girl in black stockings, juxtaposed with a sleek, powerful machine, prefigures the paintings of James Rosenquist and Peter Phillips (compare Phillips's *Custom Painting No. 5*, Plate 37). And the image of the Coca-Cola bottle is a prophecy of a famous series of paintings by Andy Warhol. While Paolozzi was living on the Continent, he met a number of important Dada artists, including Jean Arp (1886–1966) and Tristan Tzara (1896–1963), who was one of the movement's founders and the author of its manifestoes. In the spring of 1952, Paolozzi used his proto-Pop collages to illustrate a lecture for his colleagues at the Independent Group, by projecting them, rapid-fire, onto a screen using an epidiascope. Twenty years later, recognizing retrospectively the importance of his youthful collages, he published a series of facsimiles of some of them, called *Bunk*.

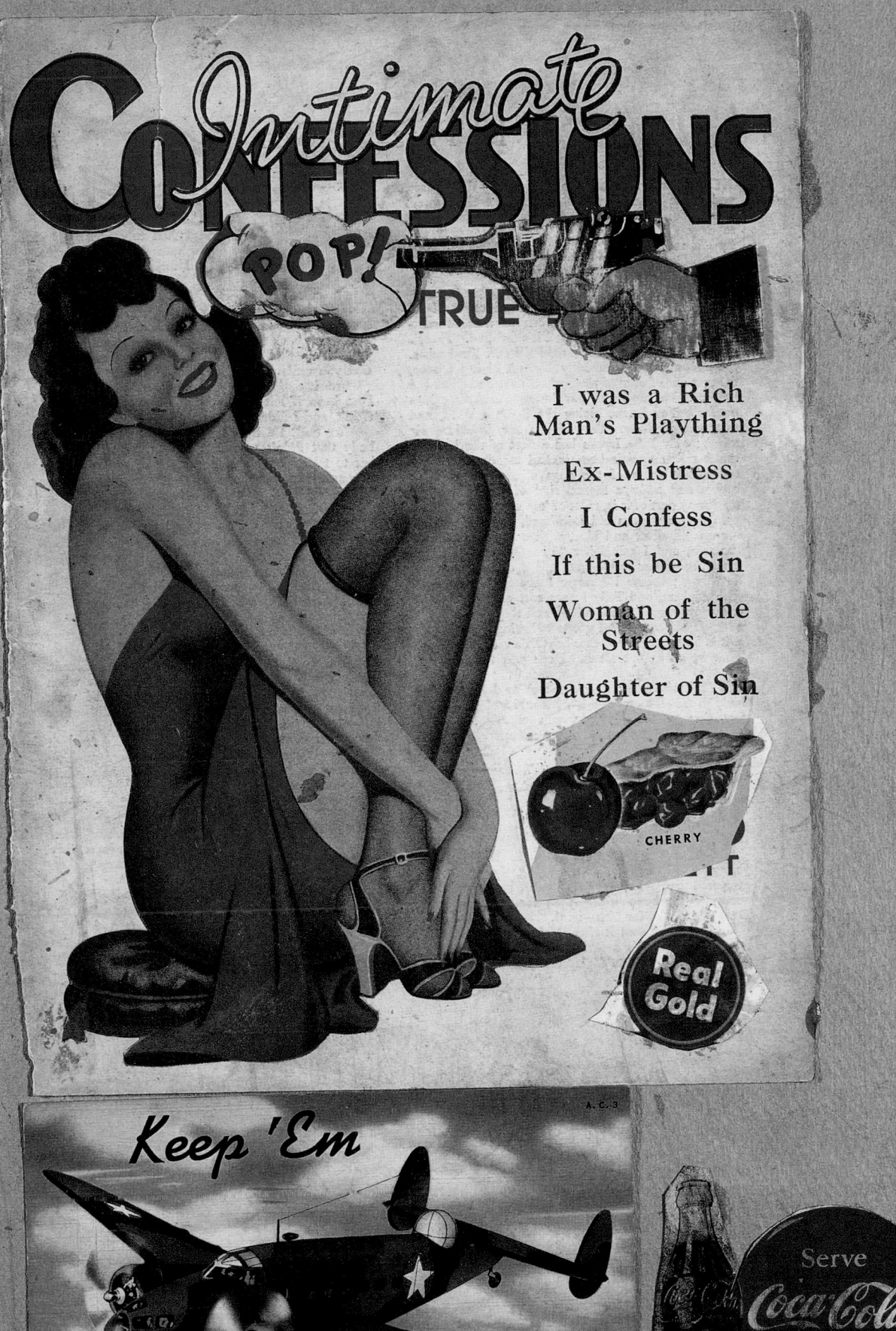

2

LARRY RIVERS (1923–)
Washington Crossing the Delaware

1953. Oil on canvas, 210.8 x 281.9 cm. Museum of Modern Art, New York

This painting is not a work of Pop Art, but it occupies a very important position in the emergence of the Pop style in America. In 1953 Rivers was one of the most successful of the younger members of the Abstract Expressionist school in New York, where the movement had nearly total control over the art scene. Yet at a time when prominent Abstract Expressionists such as Franz Kline (1910–62), Willem de Kooning and Jackson Pollock were self-conscious and intensely serious, attempting to bare their psyches in their art, Rivers chose to repaint one of the most banal American paintings, which was familiar to every schoolchild in the country through countless cheap reproductions. It was a deliberate act of outrage to apply the painterly style of Abstract Expressionism to Emmanuel Leutze's patriotic kitsch, and Rivers got exactly the response he was after: his painting was widely excoriated by the critics for its 'inappropriate' imagery and apparent disrespect of the canons of art. It was sly and ironic, and in American art in the 1950s, a sense of humour was taboo: a 'serious artist' had to be, above all, serious. The use of 'inappropriate' subject-matter, the ironic depiction of a banal image, unapologetic 'Americanness', a playful sense of humour, were all themes that would lead directly to the Pop Art movement. However, in his gestural method of applying paint to the canvas, Rivers was clearly still under the influence – whether they liked it or not – of the Abstract Expressionists.

Fig. 19
EMMANUEL LEUTZE
Washington Crossing
the Delaware
1851. Oil on canvas, 378.5
x 647.7 cm. Metropolitan
Museum of Art, New York

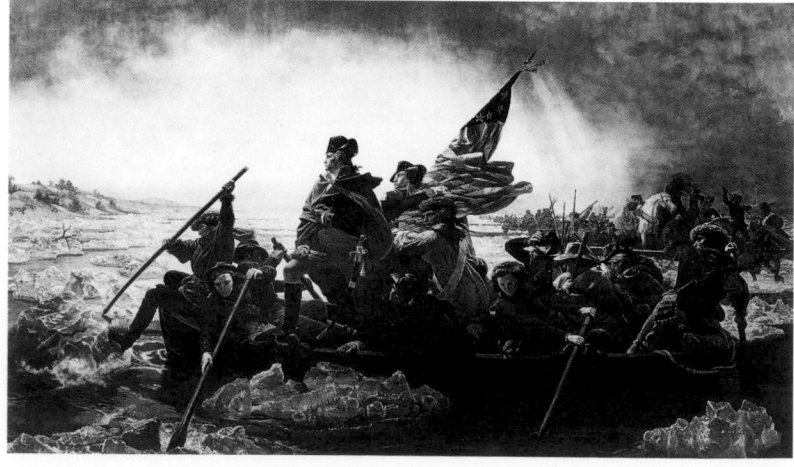

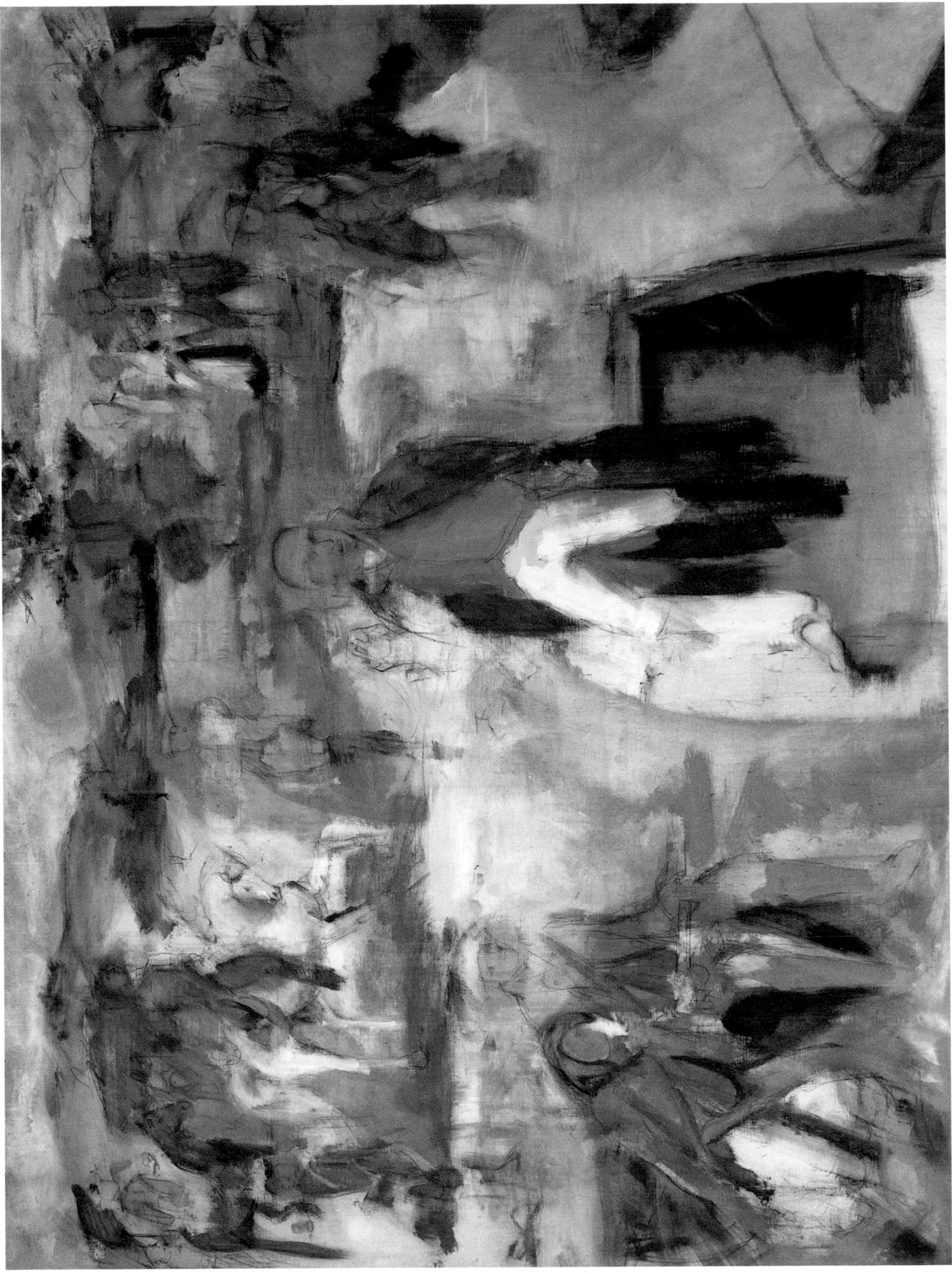

3

Jasper Johns (1930–)
Flag

1955. Encaustic, oil and collage on fabric mounted on plywood, 107.3 x 153.8 cm.
Museum of Modern Art, New York

In 1954 Jasper Johns had a dream in which he painted a large American flag. Soon after, he actually painted the work in encaustic and it became the first in a long series of flag paintings. He later commented: 'Using the design of the American flag took care of a great deal for me, because I didn't have to design it.' It was a revolutionary act: not only was the painting considered to be vaguely unpatriotic in a very patriotic era, but it was also regarded as anti-art. If the artist was not in the business of designing new images, then what was he doing? Johns, always cryptic in his public comments, had a ready reply: 'I am just trying to look for a way to make pictures.' By choosing an object so familiar to the viewer, he had freed his painting from the need to have any message or content of its own, thereby drawing attention to the process of painting itself. The simplicity and cool elegance of the painting were remarkable; Abstract Expressionism, the ruling ethos of the day, held that the highest purpose of art was to communicate the artist's deepest thoughts and feelings; in *Flag*, Johns set that dictum on its ear, and quietly suggested that a work of art need not express anything at all, except itself.

One year later, unaware of Johns's painting, Andy Warhol also painted his own *Flag*, in the highly stylized manner of his commercial illustrations at that time, although it was probably not intended to be displayed as a work of fine art. See also Claes Oldenburg's *USA Flag* (Fig. 16), which was certainly created with Johns's flag paintings in mind.

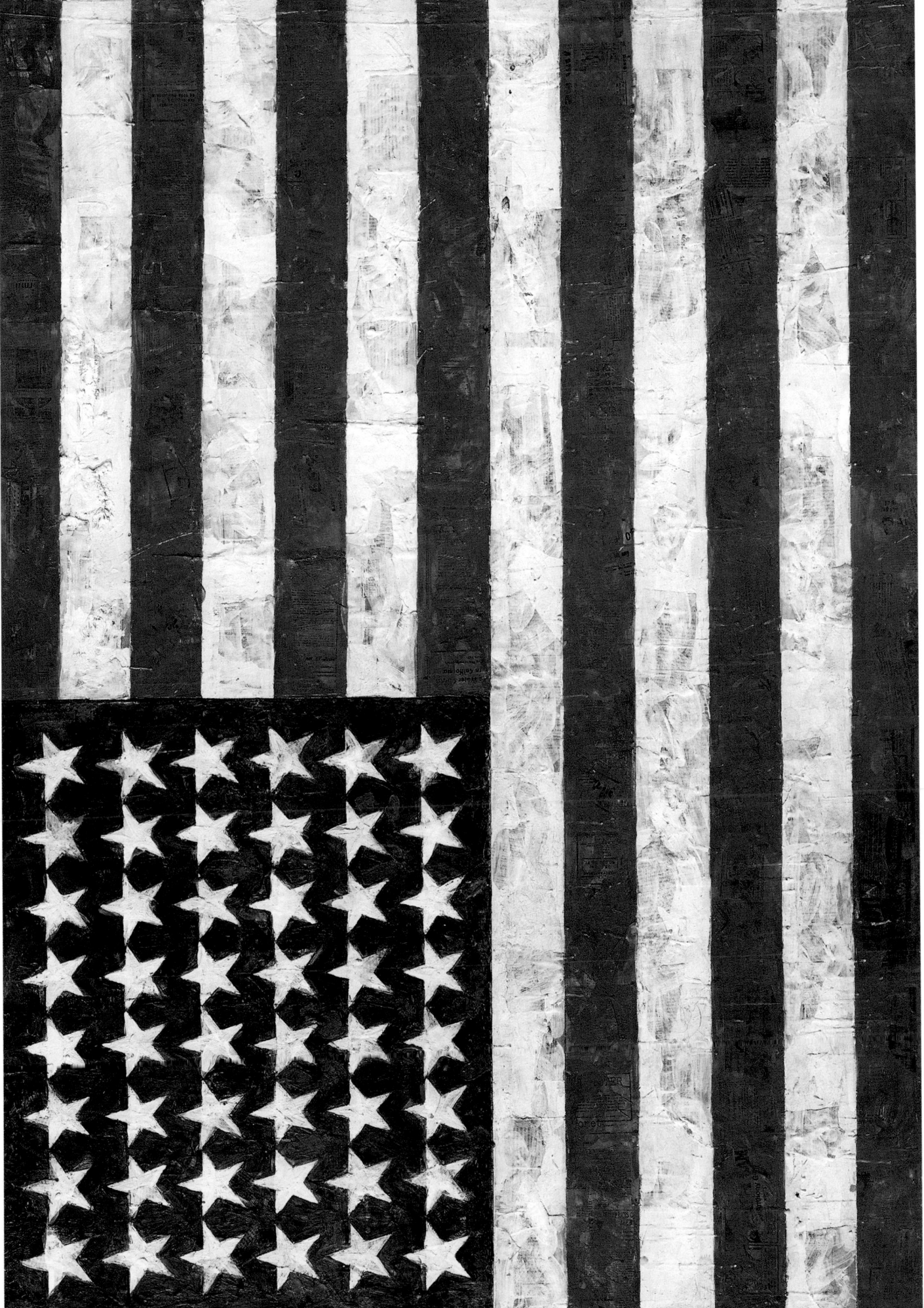

4

ROBERT RAUSCHENBERG (1925–)
Bed

1955. Combine painting, 191.1 x 80 x 20.3 cm. Museum of Modern Art, New York

Rauschenberg was intent upon pushing the limits of anti-art further and further, although many of his most outrageous works were not known beyond his immediate circle. Most outrageous of all was the *Erased de Kooning Drawing* of 1953. With the permission of Willem de Kooning, he did exactly what the title says: he completely erased a drawing by the older artist, and framed it. Whereas previous anti-art movements, notably Dada, had made their assaults on the citadel of art by using non-art materials to create articles that were deliberately ugly, or at least that had no intention of being beautiful, the *Erased de Kooning Drawing* was an act of pure nihilism, which denied the right of art even to exist. Hardly less revolutionary was *Bed*, the result of a spontaneous act of creation. The artist woke up one morning, and, deciding that he need look no further for a place to make art, he poured paint over his bedclothes and pillow. The result is a good example of what the American critic Paul Schimmel has called 'the faked gesture', a reference to one of the basic modes of expression of the Abstract Expressionists. Yet whereas the gesture for the Abstract Expressionists arose from within the artist, revealing unplumbed depths of his psyche, in Rauschenberg's view it was merely a decorative accident, with no more meaning than a house-painter's drips and blobs.

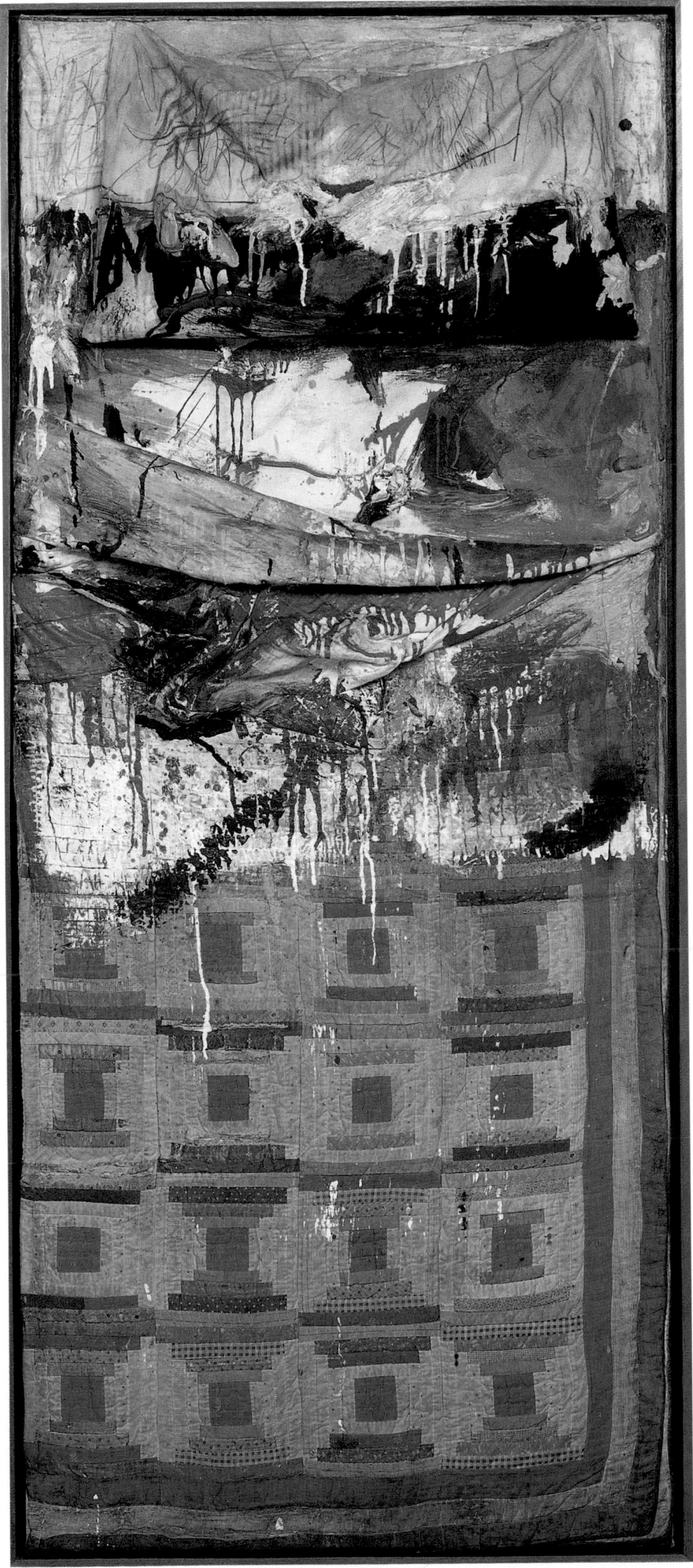

PETER BLAKE (1932–)
On the Balcony

1955–7. Oil on canvas, 121.3 x 90.8 cm. Tate Gallery, London

Peter Blake emerged as a Pop artist independent of the movement in London. Born and raised in Kent, he developed a strong interest in American Pop culture and utilized its imagery in his work from his youth. Although he studied at the Royal College of Art from 1953 to 1956, Blake's art has retained an element of the folkish throughout his career. *On the Balcony* depicts art students, the artist's classmates at the RCA, seated on a park bench, surrounded by their paintings. Commerical products such as cigarette packs, magazines, food wrappers and other litter lie around them. The frontal pose of the figures, which are presented with objects that proclaim their allegiances (an 'I love Elvis' badge, images of the British Royal Family), suggest a connection with Renaissance portraiture.

At the same time or slightly before American Pop artists were doing so, Blake was using real objects for representational ends. In *Girlie Door* (Private collection), for example, he pasted pin-ups of famous actresses and models onto a real door. More than almost any other Pop artist, Blake embraced popular culture with uncomplicated forthrightness. In works such as *Kim Novak Wall* (Private collection), painted in 1959, Blake extolled famous personalities from the popular culture several years before Andy Warhol and James Rosenquist did so. However, whereas the American artists freighted their presentations of famous actors and pop stars with irony, Blake comes across almost as a fan; the viewer has no reason to doubt that the figure wearing the badge (as well as the artist) does, in fact, love Elvis. In the 1960s, Blake himself became an influential part of the popular culture, producing posters and album covers for rock groups, notably the elaborate cover for the Beatles, *Sgt Pepper's Lonely Hearts Club Band*, in 1967. In 1975 he helped to found the Brotherhood of Ruralists, a modern equivalent of such idealistic nineteenth-century movements as the Arts and Crafts Movement.

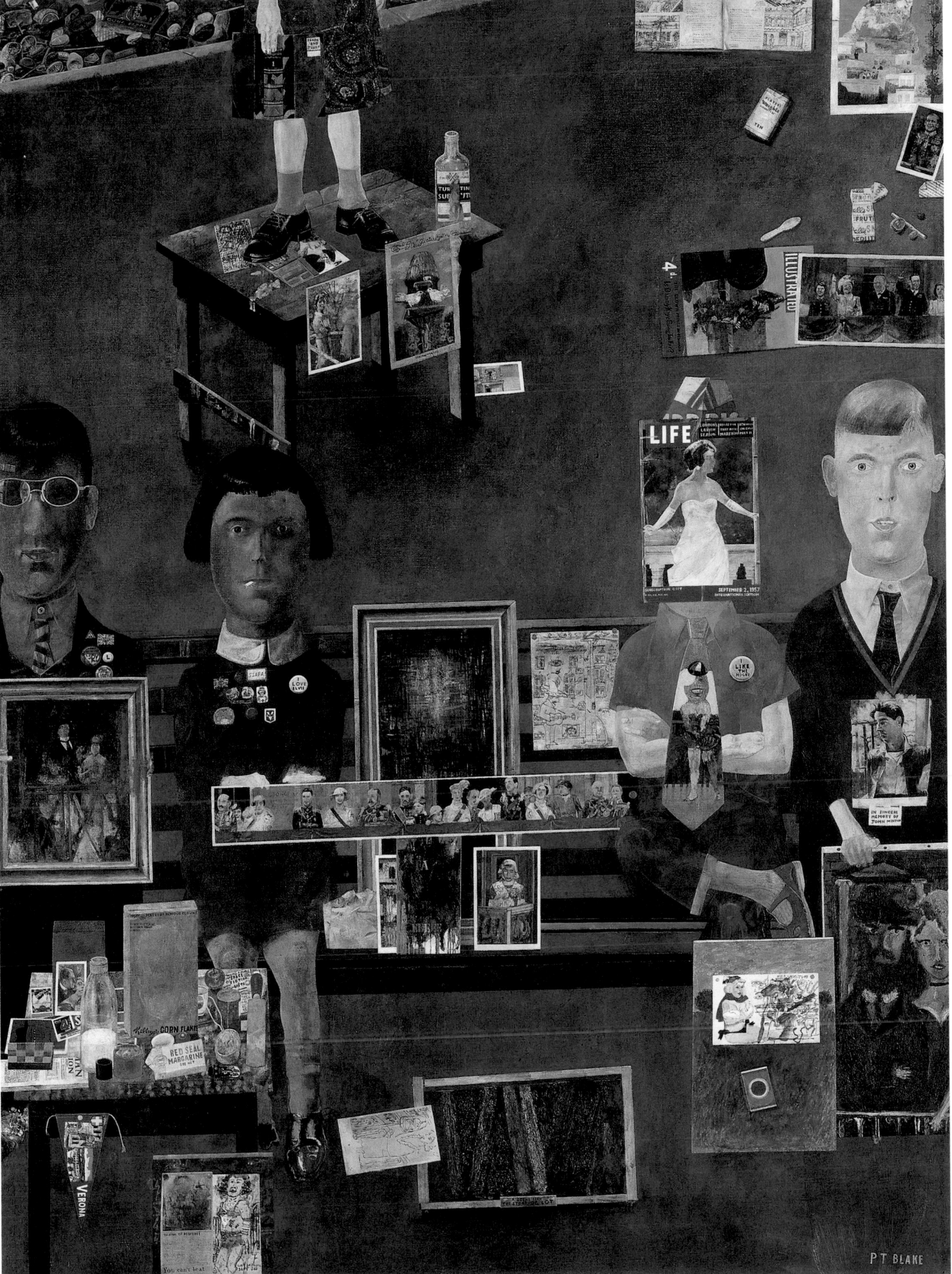

ROBERT RAUSCHENBERG (1925–)
Odalisque

1955–8. Construction, 205.7 x 63.5 x 63.5 cm. Museum Ludwig, Cologne

Even more shocking than the paintings of Jasper Johns were the breakthrough works of Robert Rauschenberg, who went one step further: if art was not anything but an object like any other, then it followed that any object at all might qualify as the raw material of art. But a stuffed chicken? A photograph of girls from a nudist magazine? Rauschenberg's junk aesthetic is directly descended from Dada (see, for example, Fig. 6), which took as its guiding principle the notion that absolutely anything under the sun could be made into art, by the merest act of transformation – or even with no transformation at all but simply by the artist's fiat. The widely disparate objects which constitute *Odalisque* have nothing in common except that they are parts of *Odalisque*; their randomness is an essential component of the work. Rauschenberg, a tall, handsome Texan with a personal manner as outspoken as his work, took New York by storm in the 1950s with works such as this one. Although he predictably provoked a great deal of criticism, he and Jasper Johns, with whom he was closely associated both personally and professionally, soon established themselves as the most important and widely imitated artists in New York. The two men were regarded as heroes by the younger generation of Pop artists. In 1962, Andy Warhol executed a series of portraits of Rauschenberg; in *Young Rauschenberg 1* (Private collection) the subject appears as a baby, surrounded by his family.

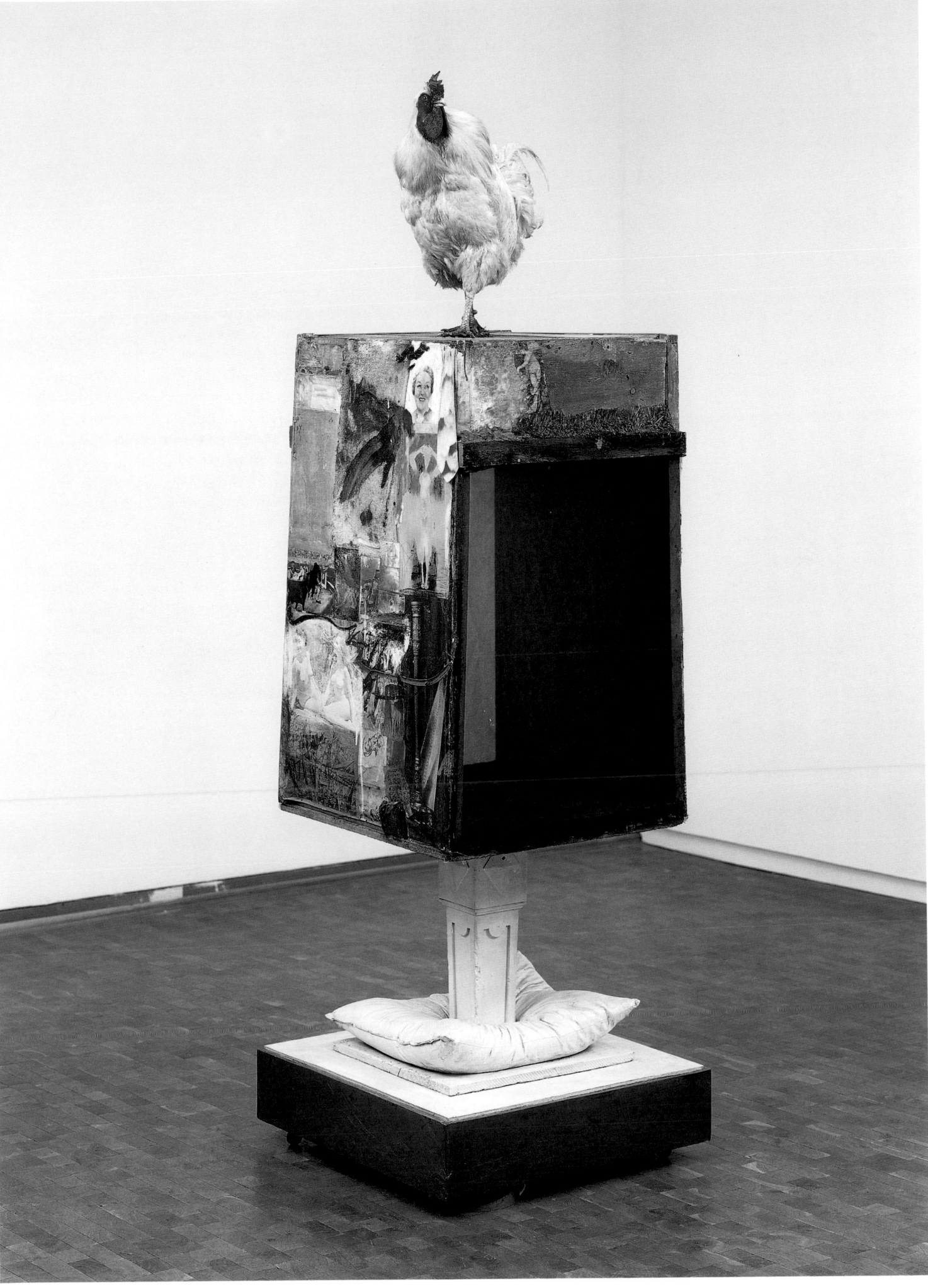

Richard Hamilton (1922–)
Just What Is It That Makes Today's Homes So Different, So Appealing?

1956. Collage, 26 x 25 cm. Kunsthalle, Tübingen

Most historians of modern art point to this little collage as the first *echt* work of Pop Art, although influential American paintings such as Jasper Johns's *Flag* (Plate 3) and Rauschenberg's *Bed* (Plate 4) predate it slightly. Designed as a poster for the landmark exhibition *This Is Tomorrow* at the Whitechapel Art Gallery, the collage neatly summarizes all the principal themes of the emergent Pop style: exaggerated sexuality, both male and female; the banality of the American middle class; popular entertainment, in the form of the comic strip and Hollywood cinema; and advanced technology. Although the television set and the reel-to-reel tape recorder in the collage have since taken on rather a quaint appearance, in 1956 they were the latest electronic appliances for the home. It is also significant that the work prominently featured the word 'POP', on the piece of candy held by the man. If *I Was a Rich Man's Plaything* (Plate 1) was the first work by an artist to include the word, *Just What Is It...*, a much more carefully finished collage than Paolozzi's, was the first publicly exhibited work to do so. While the phrase Pop Art had already been coined (perhaps by the critic Lawrence Alloway), at this early stage it was used as a slang term which referred to the popular culture which was the source of such images, not to the nascent art movement.

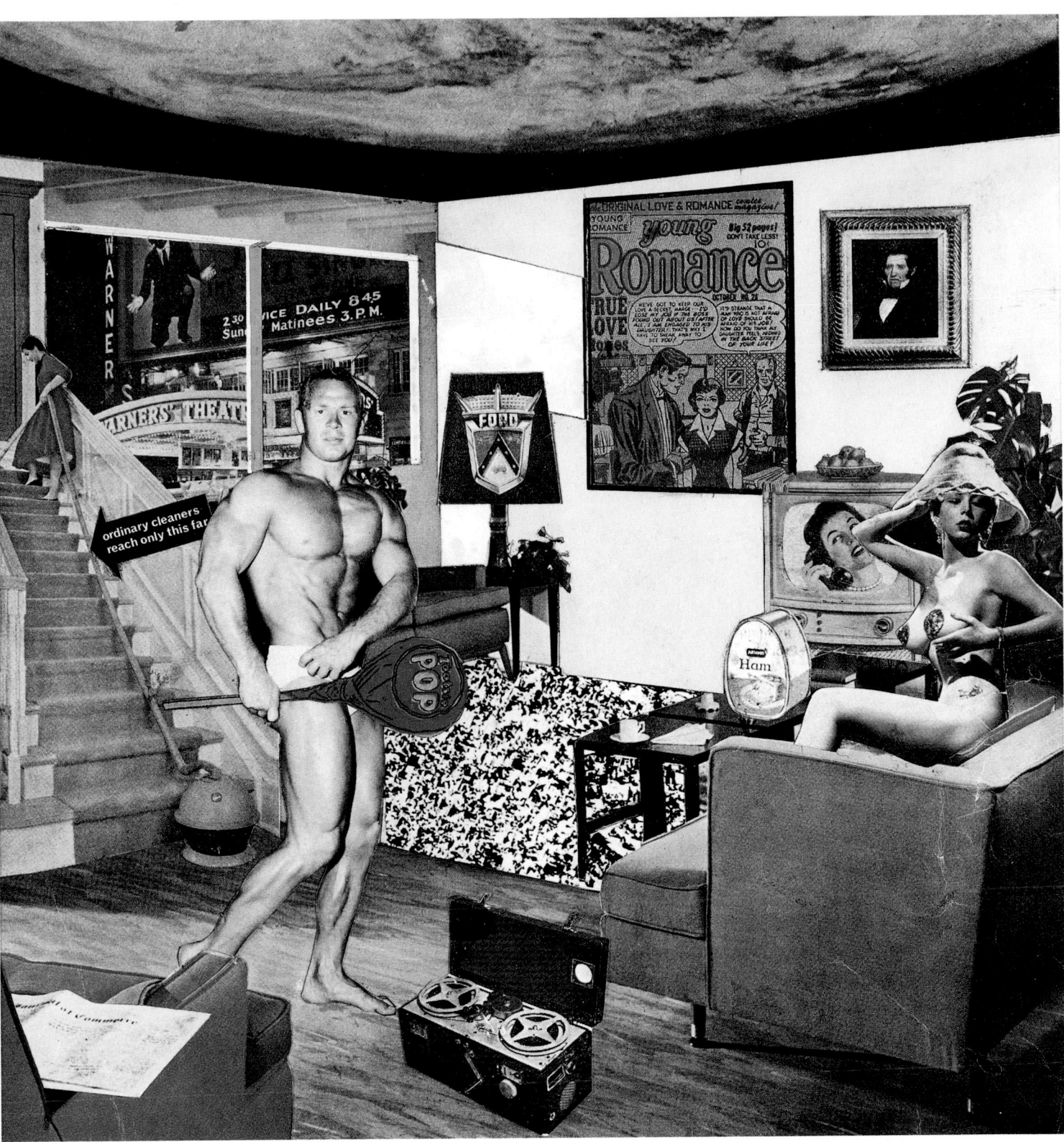

8

WAYNE THIEBAUD (1920–)
Store Window

1957. Oil on board, 27.9 x 30.5 cm. Private collection

This Northern Californian artist was among the first American painters to exploit commercial subject-matter and use it as the primary focus of his art, specializing in glossy, colourful window displays. Like Jasper Johns, he was especially interested in the fleshy presence of his paintings' surfaces. He once described his working method in these words: 'I like to see what happens when the relationship between paint and subject-matter comes as close as I can get it – white, gooey, shiny, sticky oil paint [spread] out on top of a painted cake to "become" frosting. It is playing with reality – making an illusion which grows out of an exploration of the properties of materials.' This early canvas, with its rich, sumptuous handling of the paint, shares some formal similarities with the West Coast school of Abstract Expressionism, and particularly with the region's finest artist of the 1950s, Richard Diebenkorn (1922–). Extremes of light and shade are rendered in bold geometric shapes, and the palette tends to favour pure colours or shades very high in value. Although Thiebaud's work sometimes seems closer to Dutch genre paintings of commercial scenes than it does to classic Pop Art, he was widely influential among the younger generation of Pop artists in California.

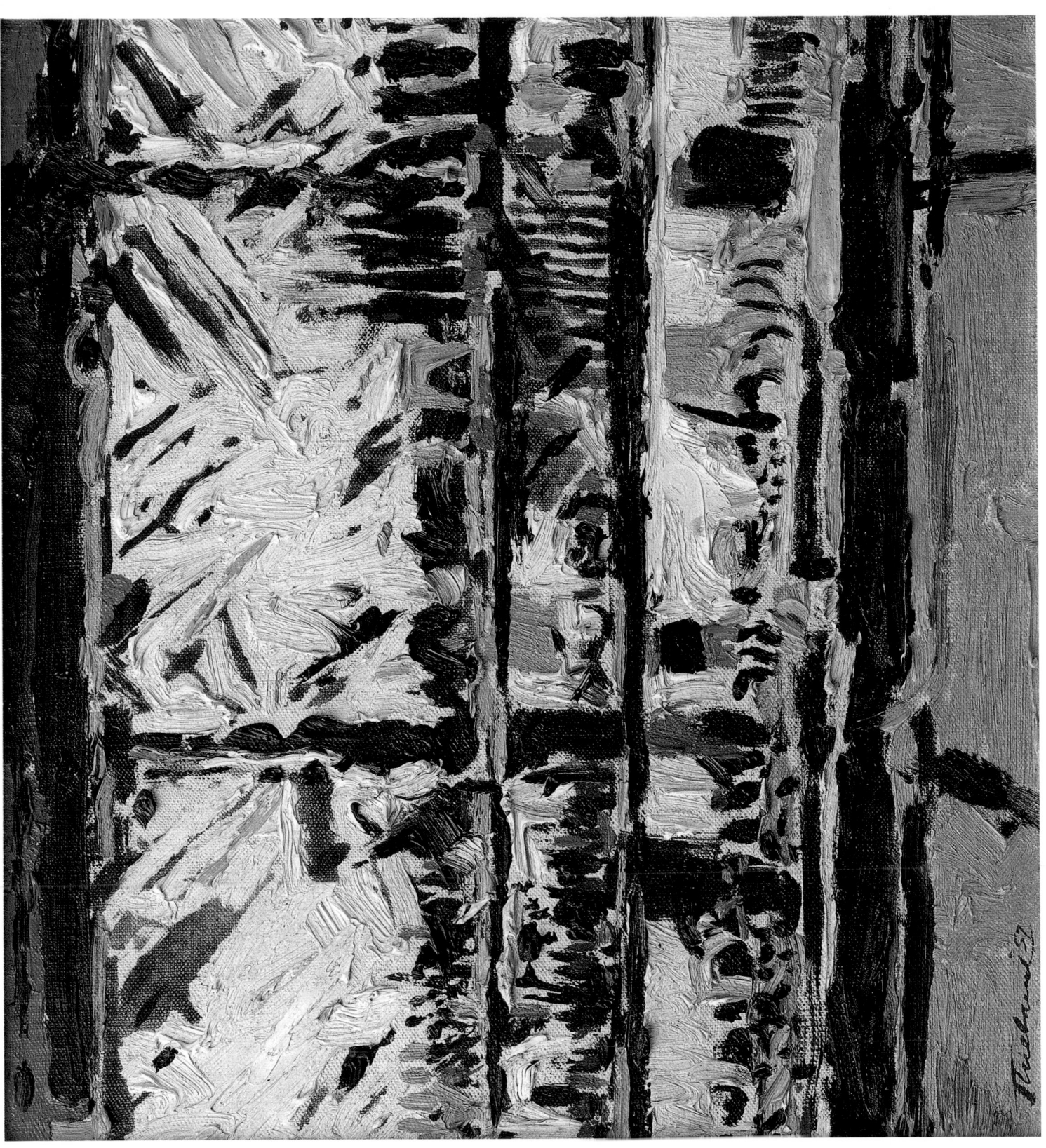

9

Jasper Johns (1930–)
White Numbers

1958. Encaustic on canvas, 170.2 x 125.8 cm. Museum Ludwig, Cologne

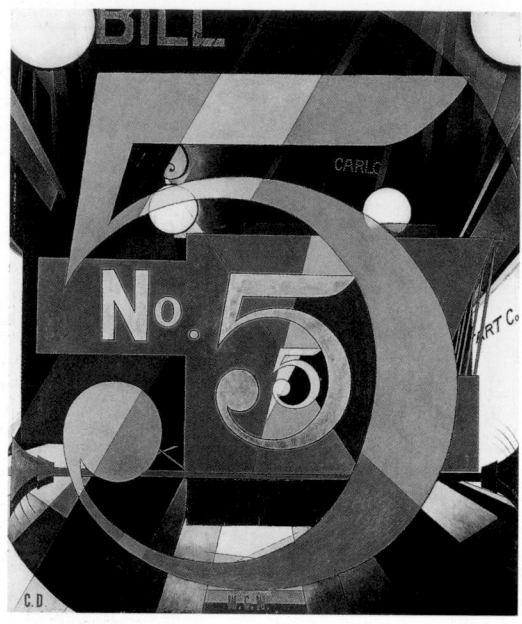

Fig. 20
Charles Demuth
I Saw the Figure 5
in Gold
1928. Oil on canvas, 90.2 x
76.2 cm. Metropolitan Museum
of Art, New York

In his numbers series, painted with industrial stencils, Johns first began to incorporate symbolic texts with his paintings. As in *Flag* (Plate 3), he chose a subject so familiar as to be almost devoid of meaning. In fact it challenged the very notion of 'meaning' in art: numbers are used to express thousands of different concepts, from how many spoons of sugar one wants in a cup of tea to the advanced mathematics of aerospace science, but the numerals have no meaning by themselves. It was precisely that quality that attracted Johns. He was certainly aware of Charles Demuth's *I Saw the Figure 5 in Gold* (Fig. 20), for one of his earliest number paintings, executed in 1955, was an homage to it entitled *Figure 5*. Although Demuth was alluding to a poem by William Carlos Williams, his painting nonetheless clearly prefigured the concept of a work of art in which the 'content' is subordinated to the design elements.

When the number paintings were first exhibited, controversy broke out about Johns's use of stencils: it was widely thought that painting numbers was one thing, but the artist ought at least to have the imagination to design them himself, rather than relying on industrial stencils. The critic Michael Crichton has recorded this typically enigmatic exchange on the subject with Johns:

Q: You nearly always use this same type. Any particular reason?
A: That's how the stencils came.
Q: But if you preferred another typeface, would you think it improper to cut your own stencils?
A: Of course not.
Q: Then you really do like these best?
A: Yes.

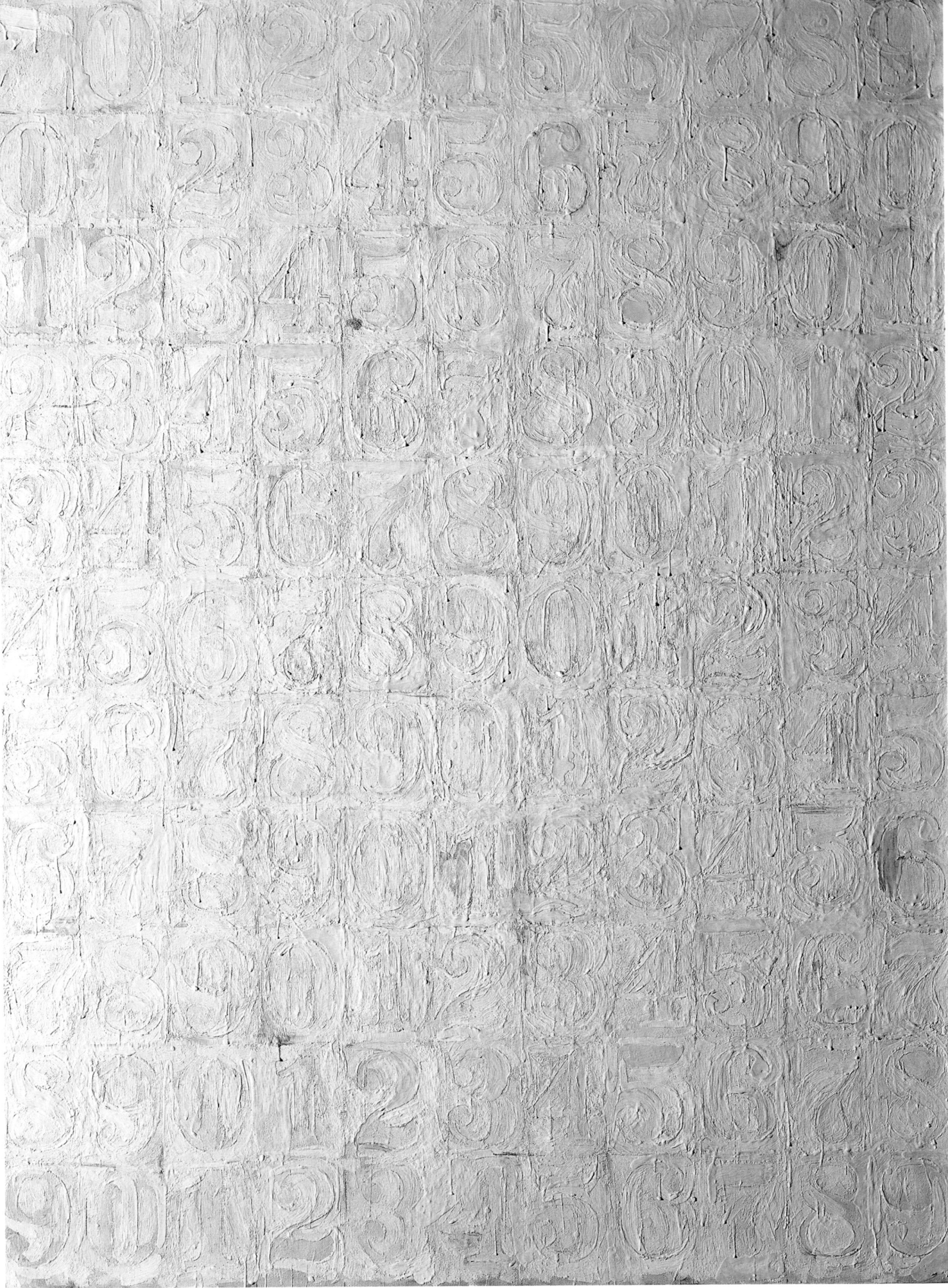

10

Billy Al Bengston (1934–)
Count Dracula II

1960. Oil on canvas, 121.9 x 121.9 cm. Newport Harbor Art Museum, Newport Beach

A native of Kansas, Billy Al Bengston attended high school and college in Los Angeles, where he supported himself at one point by working as a beach boy. He began his career as a potter, working with, among others, Kenneth Price and Peter Voulkos, who created a Californian ceramics renaissance in the early 1950s. After being expelled from several Californian art schools, he finally turned to painting in 1957. An enthusiastic biker, Bengston devoted some early canvases to various parts (and finally, in 1961, to the whole) of his motorcycle. He was among the very first artists on the American West Coast to reject the Abstract Expressionist aesthetic, and to paint in a style that was objective and yet wholly original. While he was in some ways the beau ideal of the California male, living the free and easy life of the beach, he derived much of his inspiration from the New York school. 'I believed in the lessons of the New York artists, particularly de Kooning,' he said. 'That's where I came into the picture. What their paintings said and what they verbalized was complete openness, so within that openness I began making my own paintings.' In 1958 Bengston first saw the encaustic flag and target paintings by Jasper Johns. He began a series of works based upon simple emblems, such as the Swiss cross, chevrons, the outline of a heart and the profile of an iris, as in *Count Dracula II*. These emblems have an esoteric meaning for the artist; the emblem of the iris, he has said, represents the moment when the vampire transforms himself from a bat into human shape.

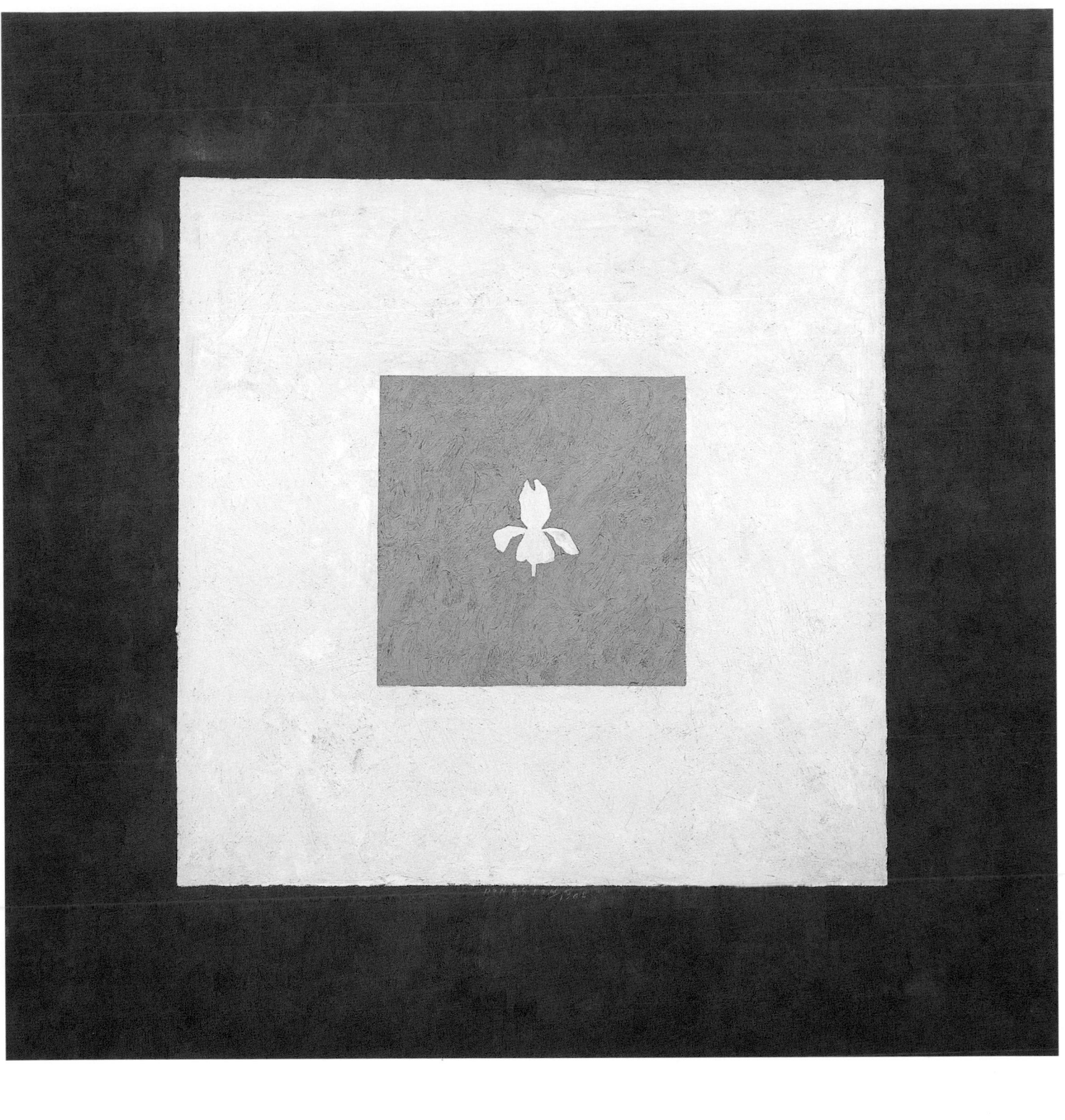

11

R.B. KITAJ (1932–)
The Murder of Rosa Luxemburg

1960. Oil and collage on canvas, 152.5 x 152.5 cm. Tate Gallery, London

Although art historians routinely include among the roster of Pop artists the name R.B. Kitaj, the American-born painter who made his name as an artist in Britain, he is probably the most conventional artist represented in this volume. One reason Kitaj is generally included among the ranks of the Pop artists is historical: he was the eldest member of the class at the Royal College of Art that produced Britian's best known Pop artists, including Patrick Caulfield and David Hockney. Another reason is his strong reliance throughout his career on found images, such as this imaginative reconstruction of the death of the founder of the German Communist Party, which employs documents and other collage elements. Like many of Kitaj's paintings, this one has a clear political message, arising in part from his strongly affirmed identity as a Jew – something which set him well apart from the mainstream of Pop Art, which as a rule kept any messages it might have ambiguous, if not muddled.

At various points in Kitaj's career, he has painted pictures that incorporated images of film stars, baseball players and famous artists and poets (although many of these were straightforward portraits). In 1973, he painted a diptych of Batman and Superman, the two popular American comic-strip heroes. However, Kitaj transformed the images completely, using them for very personal ends. The figure of Batman echoes a portrait of Beethoven, while that of Superman, which resembles David Hockney, is based upon a drawing of the comic-book hero by a psychotic child.

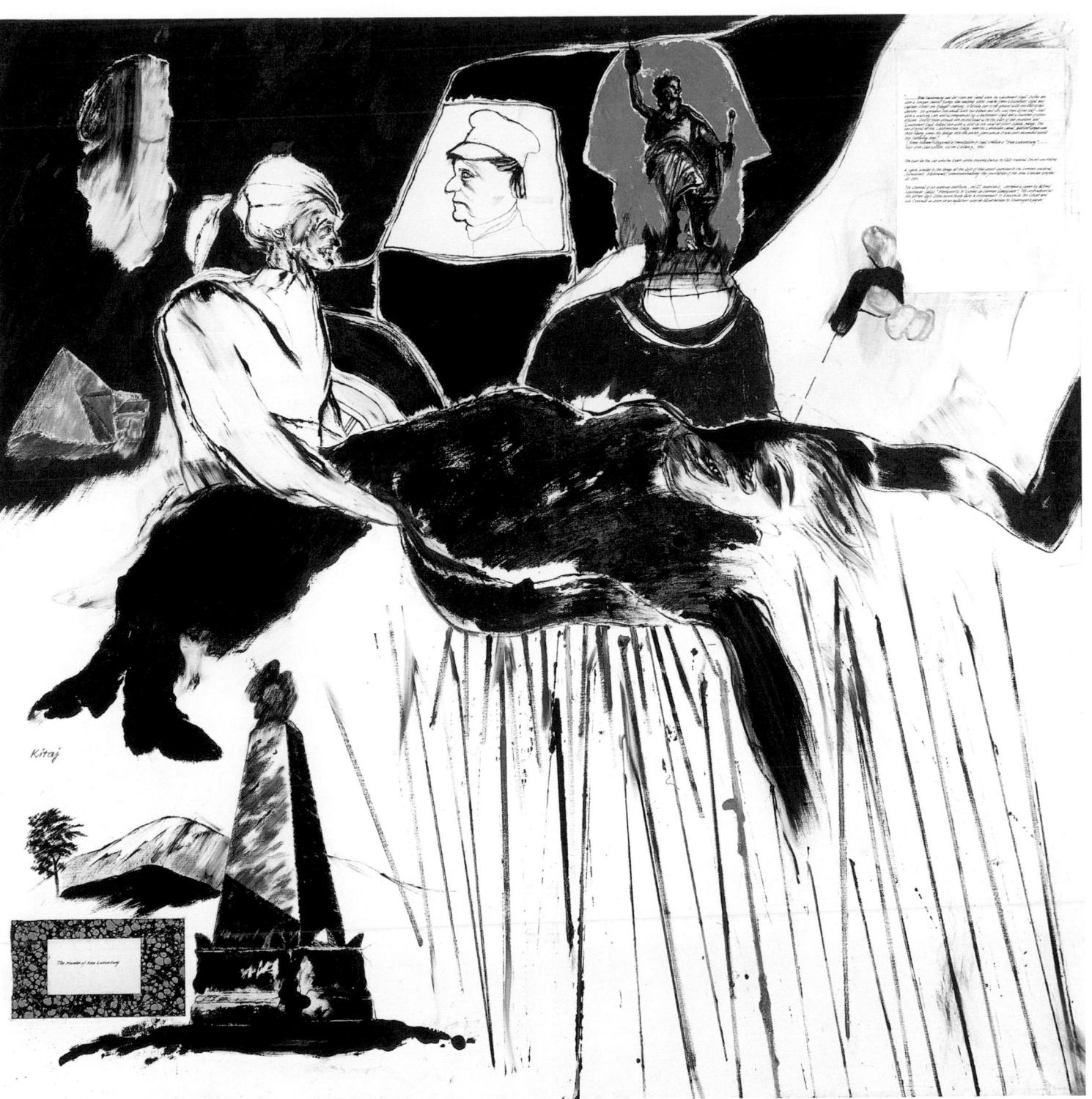

Kitaj

The Murder of Rosa Luxemburg

12

JAMES ROSENQUIST (1933–)
President Elect

1960–1. Oil on masonite, 226.1 x 505.5 cm. Musée Nationale d'Art Moderne, Paris

James Rosenquist's credentials as a Pop artist were above reproach: in his native Minnesota he had painted billboards and signs, an employment which he continued when he moved to New York in 1957 to study fine art. After he met the luminaries of the New York art world, including Jasper Johns and Robert Rauschenberg, it was natural for him to look at the commercial painting he was doing in his day job with a critical eye. The first easel painting he did in the Pop style was *President Elect*, which juxtaposed the face of the newly elected president, John F. Kennedy, with commercial images of a slice of cake and an automobile fender. He painted these images in exactly the same cool, uninflected style that he employed in his billboards, working from a newspaper collage. The purpose of the disjointed images is not satirical, nor is it even absurdist; rather, the intended effect is one of randomness. Strongly influenced by Rauschenberg's combine paintings, Rosenquist was manufacturing, in critic Marco Livingstone's words, 'jarring juxtapositions of apparently unrelated things such as one might experience in walking or driving down a street, in flicking through the pages of a magazine or in quickly switching channels on television.'

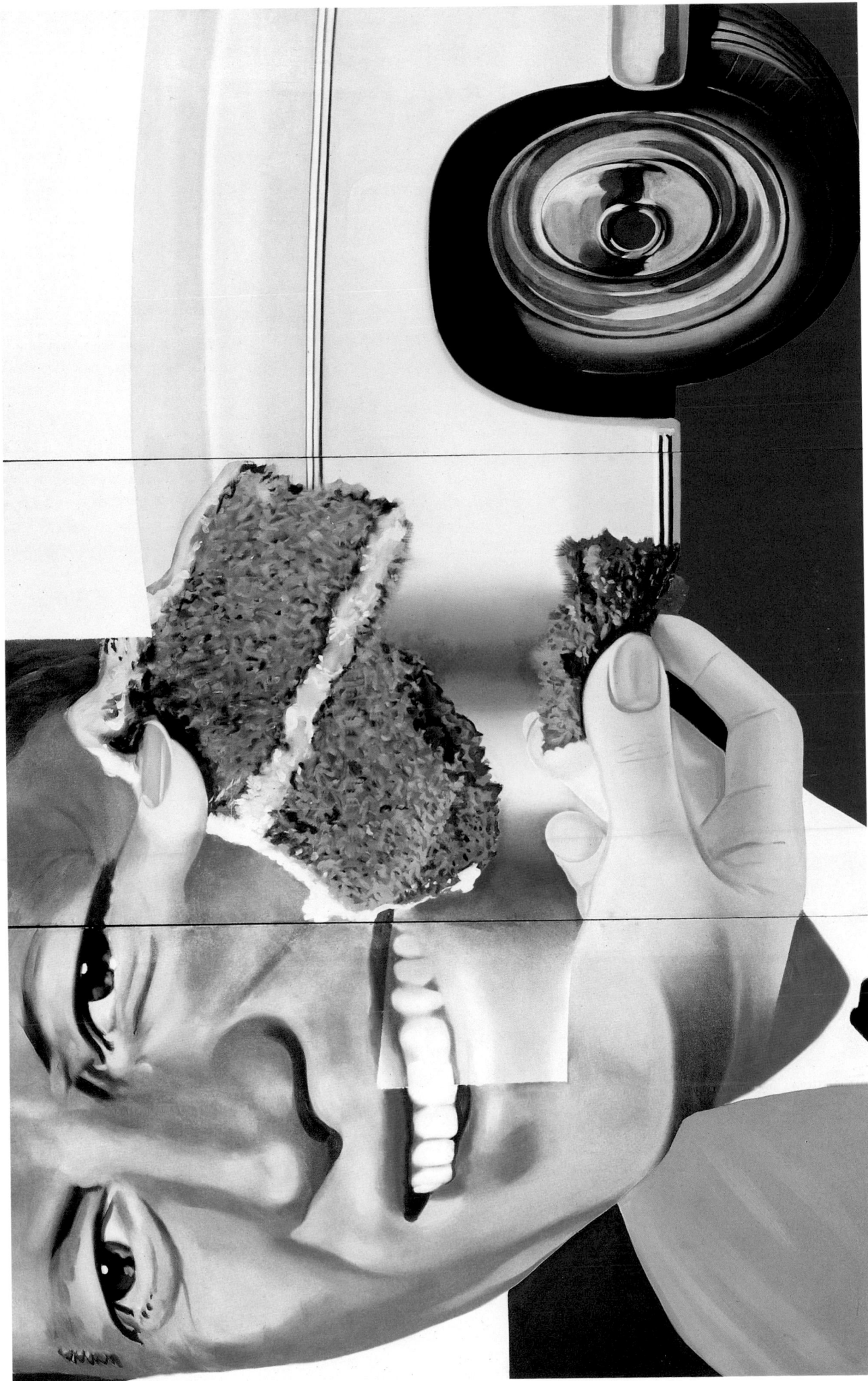

13

Peter Blake (1932–)
Self Portrait with Badges

1961. Oil on hardboard, 172.7 x 120.6 cm. Tate Gallery, London

In this self-portrait Blake forthrightly advertises himself as a lover of the American youth culture. He is dressed in American blue jeans, a denim jacket and sneakers, and holding a fan magazine devoted to Elvis Presley (one year before Andy Warhol painted his portraits of the most popular rock singer of the day). At the time, it was almost an act of defiance for the artist to identify himself so clearly with American pop culture, which was then considered by the British intelligentsia to be crass, commercial and even anti-intellectual. Wearing badges was becoming a popular form of self-expression for young people; in one of his most famous early works, *On the Balcony* (Plate 5), Blake had portrayed students wearing badges (including a young girl wearing a badge that proclaimed 'I LOVE ELVIS'). The badges in his self-portrait reinforce his association with American pop culture; among them are another Elvis badge, one from the Boy Scouts of America and political campaign badges for Adlai Stevenson and Fiorello La Guardia, the former mayor of New York. While there is no doubt that the artist's affection for all these things is genuine, a certain yearning pervades the work. By 1961 Fiorello La Guardia had been dead for fourteen years, Adlai Stevenson's last campaign for the American presidency had ended five years earlier, and even Elvis Presley had begun to lose his artistic vitality. The face that peers out at the viewer from behind all that youthful paraphernalia does not look quite young enough; there is a palpable sense that the subject is clinging to a youth that is slipping away.

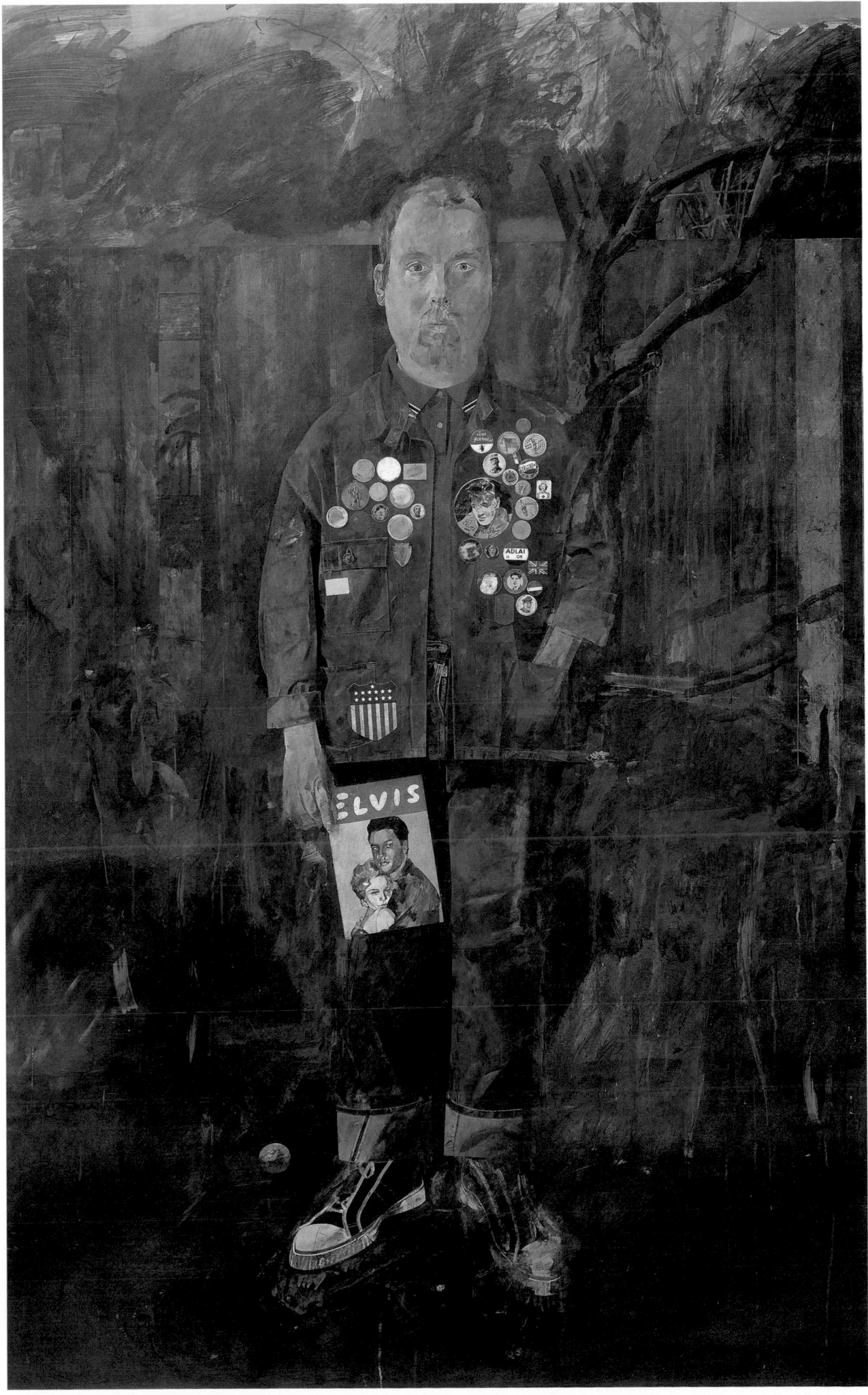

14

DAVID HOCKNEY (1937–)
Tea Painting in an Illusionistic Style

1961. Oil on canvas, 185 x 76 cm. Private collection

Like R.B. Kitaj, David Hockney produced few paintings in pure Pop style. At first glance this image of a box of cheap tea, which is painted on a shaped canvas, appears to be an attempt at a monumental representation of a commercial product common in the everyday lives of British people. Yet the loose, painterly style and the ghostly male figure which mysteriously appears to be seated inside the box, undermine the illusion – hence the title of the painting. The artist tells us that the work is in 'an illusionistic style', rather than being actually illusionistic. The jarring misspelling of the word 'tea' on the box's side panel confirms the falseness of the illusion. As the viewer looks at the painting, he has the sense of witnessing a work in the midst of becoming, as though the artist has walked away from his easel and might come back at any moment and sharpen the edges of his images, or perhaps even correct the spelling mistake. This emphasis on the process of art-making united Hockney with Johns and Rauschenberg, who were revolutionizing the American art scene with similarly problematic works.

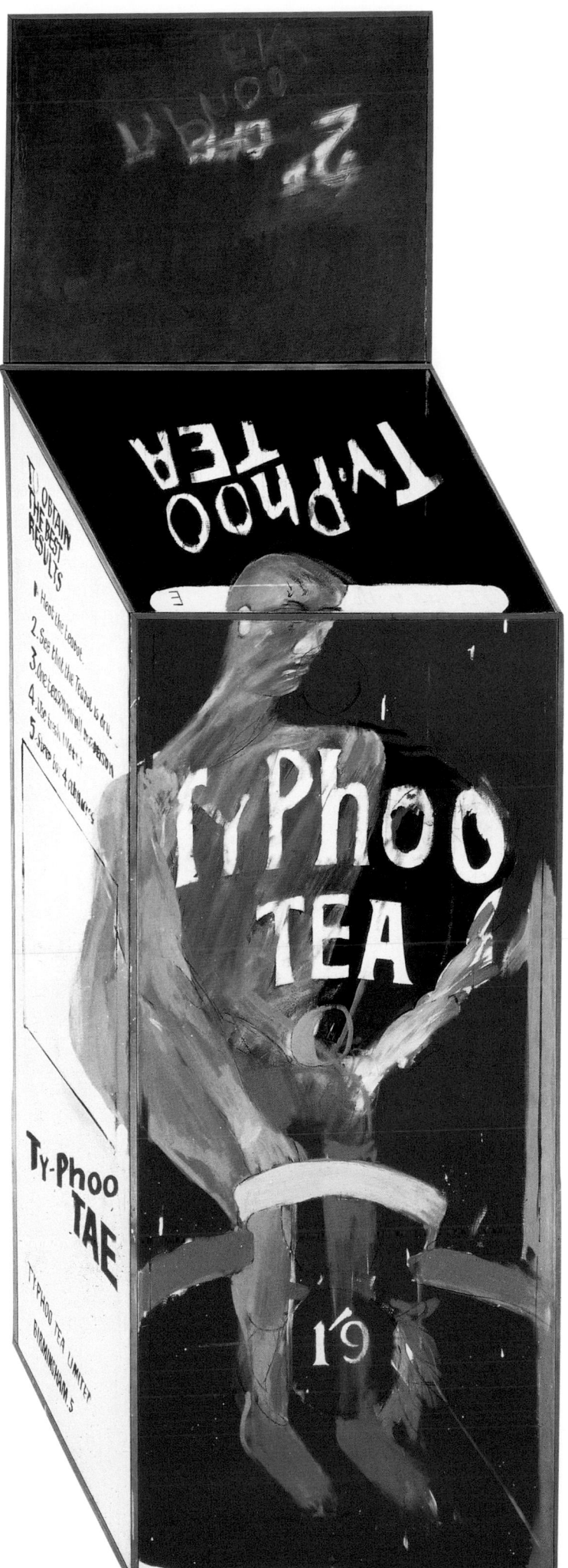

15

DAVID HOCKNEY (1937–)
The Most Beautiful Boy in the World

1961. Oil on canvas, 177.8 x 100.3 cm. Private collection

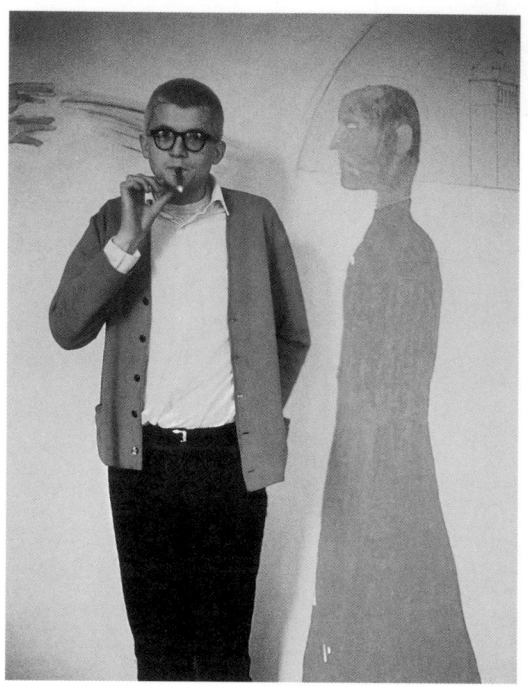

Fig. 21
LORD SNOWDON
Portrait of David
Hockney with *The
Hypnotist*, 1962–3

Hockney was openly homosexual at a time when homosexuality was not only a social taboo but also illegal in England. In several of the early paintings which established his international reputation, he employed explicit sexual themes in a way that had never been done before in a fine-art context. The title of this painting is plain enough, and yet the artist puts a playful twist on the viewer's expectations, by sketching a feminine peignoir on the figure of the boy. The numeral 69 probably refers to a sexual act, and the 'D.Boy' written on the figure's shoulder, with musical notes hovering just above it, refers to a hit tune by Cliff Richard, a handsome young pop singer who was popular with the gay set in London at that time. The Alka-Seltzer sign intrudes itself without apology or obvious pertinence to the subject (unless it is making an oblique reference to the perils of night-club-bing), as though the artist's gaze just happened to fall upon a box of the headache remedy while he was working on the painting. In 1961 it was shocking to exhibit a work of art that set forth homosexual themes so openly, and the painting has not yet entirely lost its shock value. Yet Hockney presented it with an insouciance and a charm that disarmed his critics. The artist has a great gift for self-promotion, and he became a darling of the media. By the time he left England to live in Los Angeles in 1964, he was so popular that many people who might otherwise have disapproved of him kept their thoughts to themselves, lest they be accused of prudishness.

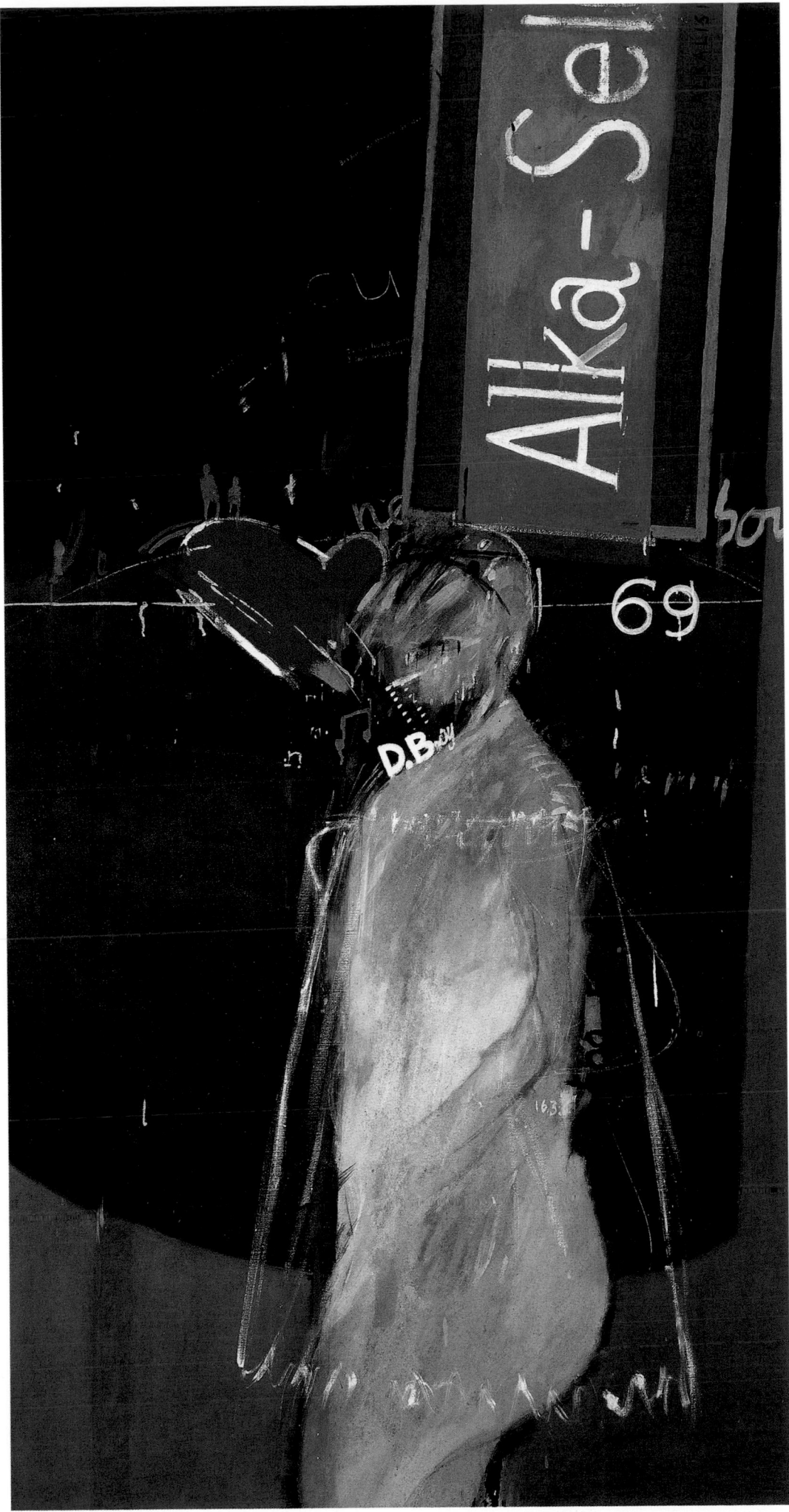

16

James Rosenquist (1933–)
I Love You with my Ford

1961. Oil on canvas, 86.4 x 91.4 cm. Moderna Museet, Stockholm

One of the distinguishing features of Rosenquist's art was his love of disorienting shifts in scale, a device he borrowed from his experience as a billboard painter. In these three panels, the scale balloons from an enormously overblown mass of spaghetti, to a rotated slice of a scene of two lovers (in black and white) only slightly enlarged, to a shrunken automobile. An enlarged image of spaghetti had already made its appearance in the very beginning of Pop Art, in the 1956 exhibition *This Is Tomorrow* at the Whitechapel Art Gallery in London. It is doubtful whether Rosenquist was aware of the earlier use of the image, but in both cases food, when used as a Pop Art image, has been made to appear quite unappetizing, like an object made of plastic. In the earlier paintings of candies and pastries by Wayne Thiebaud, the edibles have the specific gravity of lead.

While it is customary to describe these early Pop paintings of Rosenquist's (dating from 1960–2) as being devoid of both emotion and irony, there is nonetheless an element of nostalgia in many of them. Whereas other Pop painters who depicted technology in their works selected images that portrayed sleek, modern machines, Rosenquist, both here and in *President Elect* (Plate 12) chose automobiles that were some ten years out of date, implying that the American consumer culture he was capturing in his art was already passé – in much the same way that Peter Blake associated himself with a vanishing era of American popular culture in his *Self Portrait with Badges* (Plate 13).

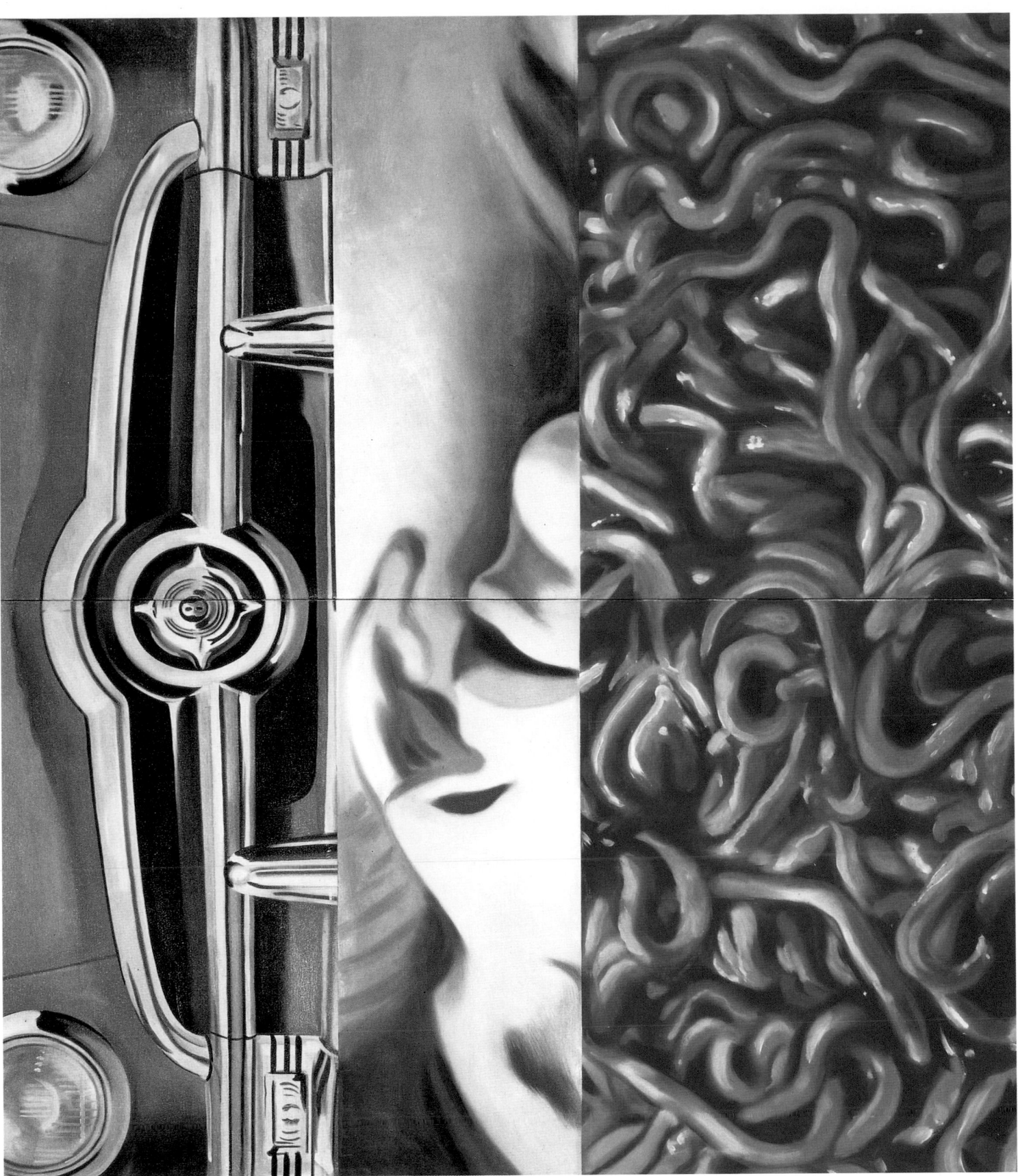

17

JOE GOODE (1937–)
Milk Bottle Painting (Two-Part Blue)

1961–2. Oil on canvas with oil on glass bottle, 174 x 167.6 cm. Private collection

The milk bottle paintings of Californian artist Joe Goode represent the final streamlining of Rauschenberg's combine painting. If Pop Art is defined as painting and other fine arts that take as their subject-matter objects and commercial products from everyday life, then Goode qualifies. However, the elegant profile of the bottle (which towards the end of the twentieth century has all but disappeared from everyday life in America) has a pristine, even classical shape, which is perhaps the reason that Goode chose it, more even than because the object relates the painting directly to the life experience of the viewer. Goode produced a large number of milk bottle paintings in the early 1960s, which vary only slightly from each other. They bear obvious formal affinities with Jim Dine's tool paintings of the same period, although Goode's painting style is far more austere. His restrained palette and cool, anti-painterly application techniques reveal the influence of the Minimalist school, as represented by painters such as Jules Olitski (1922–), Robert Ryman (1930–) and Ellsworth Kelly. Minimalism was one of Pop Art's principal 'competitors' on the American art scene at that time.

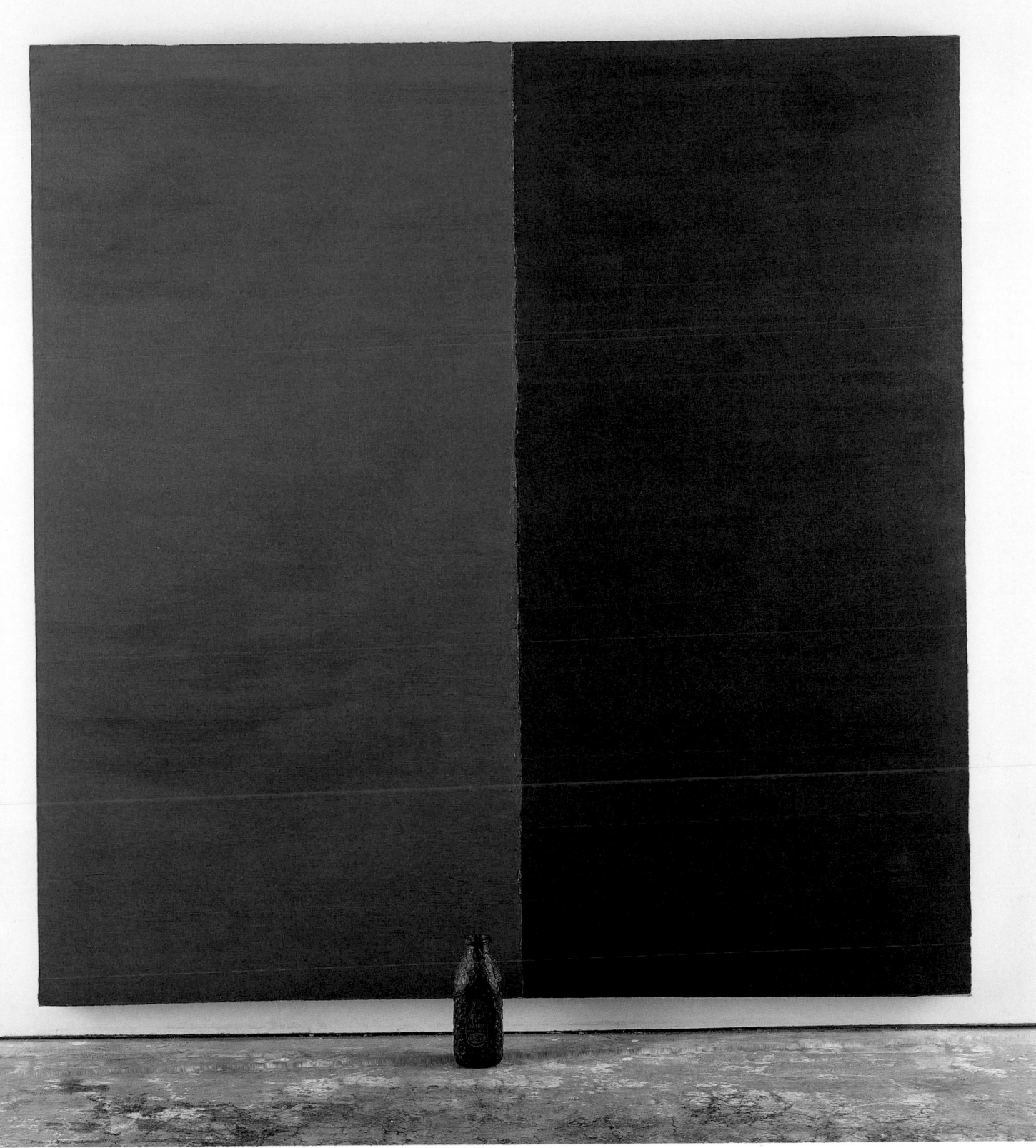

18

JIM DINE (1935–)
Child's Blue Wall

1962. Oil on canvas, wood, metal, light bulb, 152.4 x 182.9 cm. Albright-Knox Art Gallery, Buffalo, New York

A close associate of Claes Oldenburg's, Jim Dine was one of the earliest pioneers of the Happenings, public multimedia events in which the spectators were brought into direct contact with the creative process. These spontaneous, cabaret-like events flowed freely from one medium to another: poetry, theatre, dance and other performance media were loosely mixed together with painting and drawing to create works that were intended to capture the energy of the moment, very much in the spirit of Dada and Surrealism. In his paintings, Dine also strove to make as direct a connection as possible between the canvas and everyday life. In 1959, four years after Robert Rauschenberg's *Bed* (Plate 4), Dine took a suit of his clothes and heavily painted it over with oil paint, calling the work *Green Suit* (Private collection). *Name Painting (1935–63) I* (Private collection), which was painted in the years 1968–9, is a large canvas upon which the artist inscribed the names of his friends during the first twenty-eight years of his life. The paintings for which Dine is best known are those that combine images on canvas with three-dimensional objects, especially tools. *Child's Blue Wall* is an unusually lyrical work for Dine, which attempts to capture the magic of childhood and make it concrete, with the emblematic detail of a real child's lamp casting light on the canvas.

Fig. 22
ROBERT R. MCELROY
Installation photograph of *Car Crash*, a Jim Dine Happening, 1960

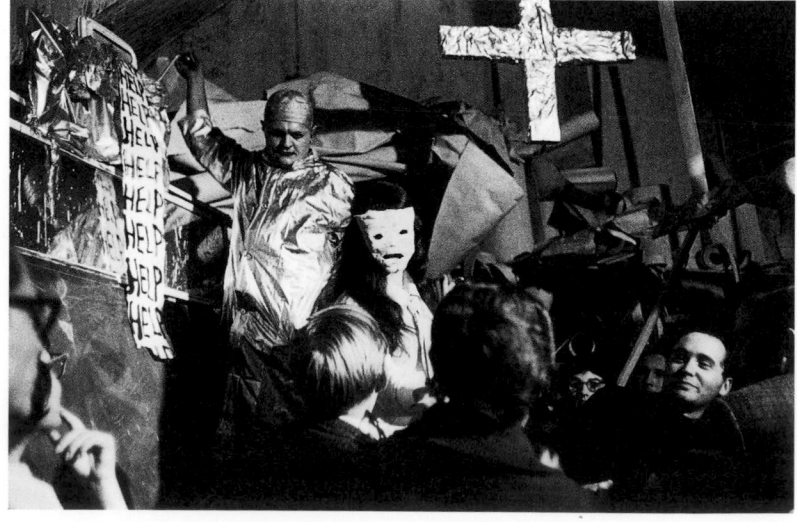

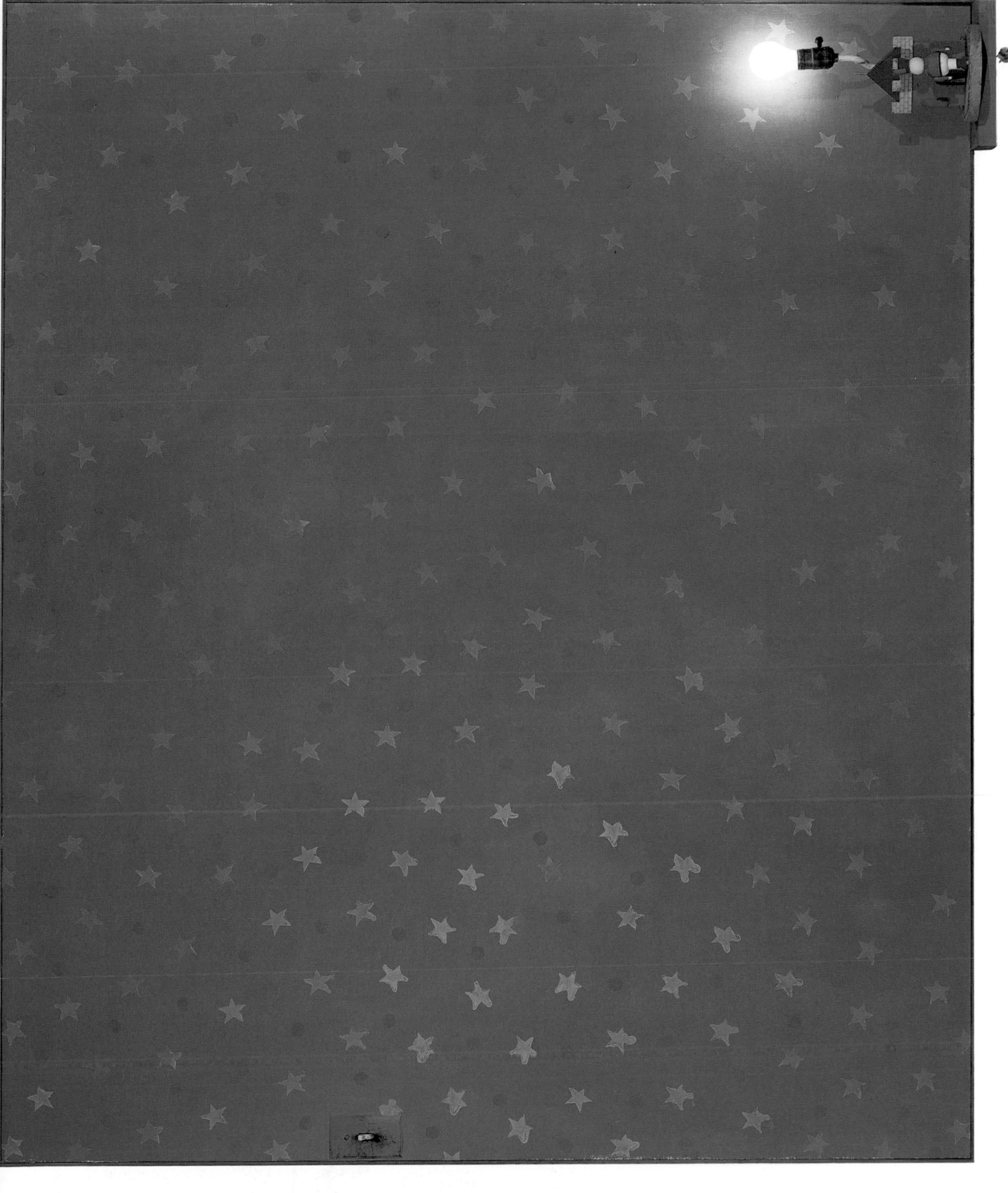

19

JASPER JOHNS (1930–)
Fool's House

1962. Oil on canvas with objects, 182.9 x 91.4 cm. Private collection

In an interview, Johns identified this work as the first of his paintings to be influenced by the philosophy of Ludwig Wittgenstein. He said that reading Wittgenstein had caused him to reject the traditional notion of meanings in art. The only intention the artist could legitimately carry out was to make art; anything more than that was suspect. Since art could only be certain of succeeding by 'being', as opposed to 'meaning', Johns placed great importance upon his materials; rather than manipulating them towards some preconceived end, he claimed that they told him what to do. The process of creation is vividly apparent in *Fool's House*, in the wiping motion revealed in the trail of paint left by the swinging broom. At first glance this work might seem to be close in spirit to the work of Abstract Expressionist action painters such as Jackson Pollock, who forcefully dripped and splashed paint onto his canvases. Yet there is a key distinction: in the case of a painting by Pollock, the gesture is that of the artist himself, but in *Fool's House* the painting motion is made by an element of the painting. The hand of the artist has been concealed. The use of everyday objects – the broom, the towel, the cup – is a direct influence from the work of Robert Rauschenberg, who incorporated all sorts of objects into his combine paintings.

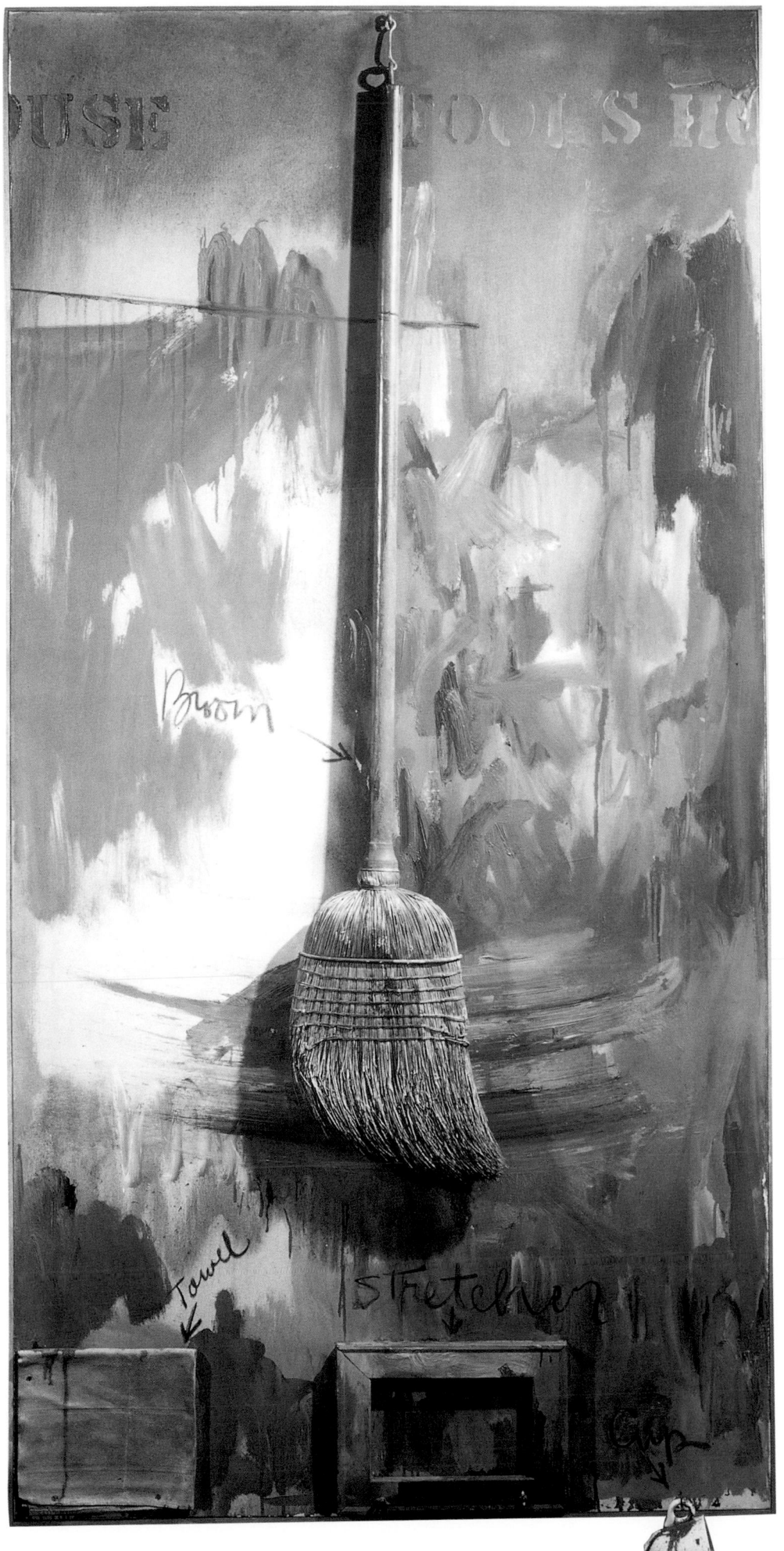

20

Roy Lichtenstein (1923–)
George Washington

1962. Oil on canvas, 129.5 x 96.5 cm. Private collection

In New York in 1961, two artists who were at the time unknown to each other began producing paintings of images borrowed from comic strips: one of them was Andy Warhol, who painted seven canvases of cartoon characters and then dropped the idea, and the other was Roy Lichtenstein, who has based his entire career upon paintings in the style of comic strips. He began with a painting of Walt Disney's creations Mickey Mouse and Donald Duck, but soon moved on to less immediately recognizable comic-strip subjects who were not famous in their own right – or, in the case of this early painting, who were not cartoon characters at all. Like Andy Warhol, Lichtenstein attempted to remove any evidence of his own hand in his paintings, and gave them a carefully crafted, machine-made appearance. He did this by mimicking the printing techniques that were used by the comic-book publishers themselves, particularly the screens of tiny dots, called Ben-Day dots, which approximate the tone of a painting. This practice resulted in a paradox: although the artists who created the original comic strips produced finished paintings, like the work of 'real artists', Lichtenstein, who was a 'real artist' in the sense that he was being exhibited in art galleries, deliberately gave his paintings the appearance of having been reproduced. Like all the American Pop artists, most of Lichtenstein's images reflected the banality of the American consumer culture: borrowing from comic books, they could hardly do otherwise. And while there is often a gentle ironical edge in his works (more so than in the case of Andy Warhol), there is also a lyrical undercurrent of affection for the American stereotypes being caricatured. While the artist here is undoubtedly making a wry, satirical point about the hackneyed images of patriotism, one senses that he is also rather fond of the stone-faced Father of his Country.

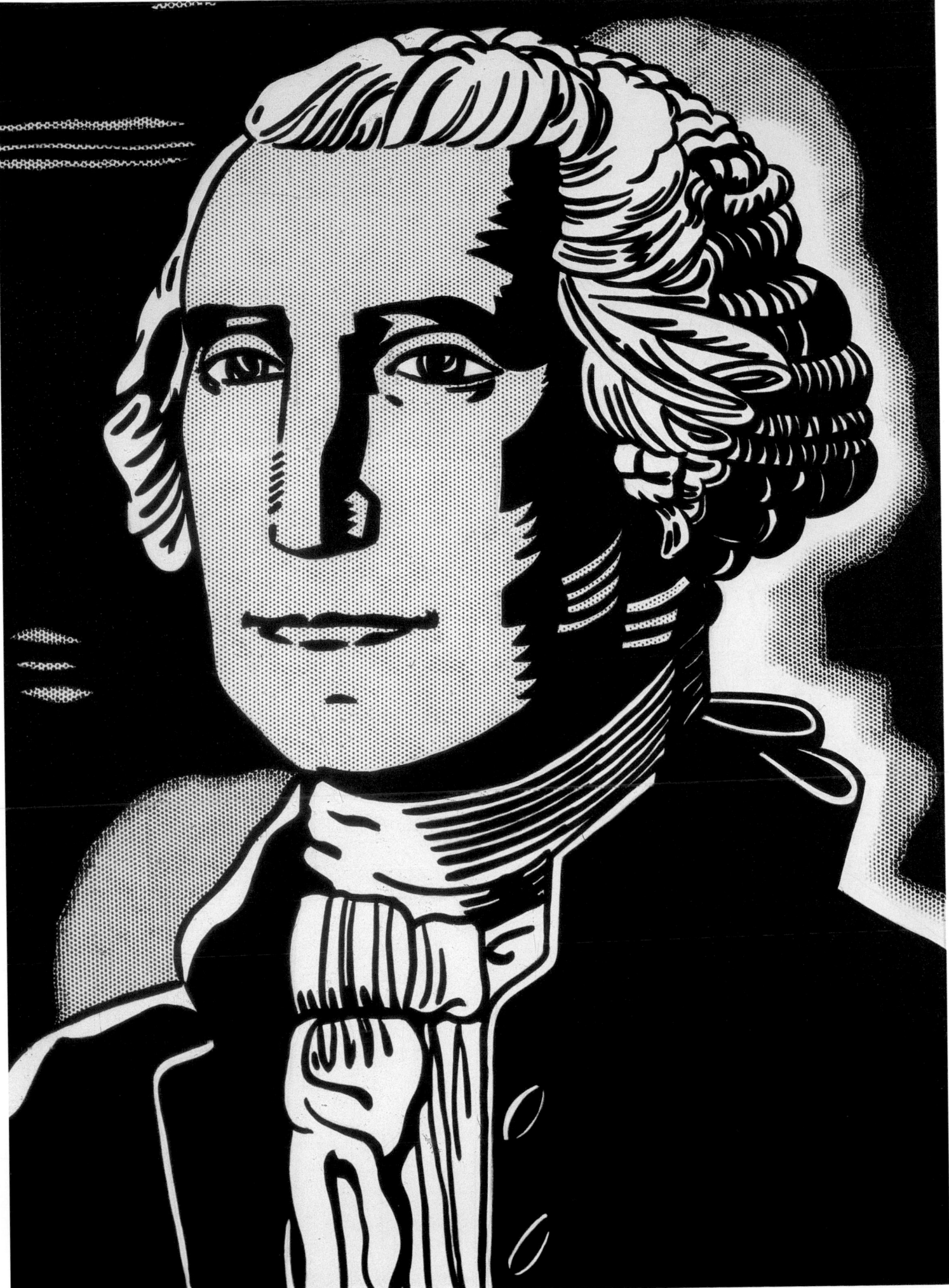

21

ANDY WARHOL (1928–86)
Big Campbell's Soup Can (19¢)

1962. Acrylic and graphite on canvas, 182.9 x 138.4 cm. The Menil Collection, Houston

Andy Warhol was trained as a commercial artist at the Carnegie Institute of Technology, Pittsburgh, and when he moved to New York in 1949, he quickly established a successful career selling illustrations to smart magazines such as *The New Yorker*, *Vogue* and *Harper's Bazaar*. Warhol painted his first easel paintings in the Pop style in 1960. Among them were canvases of Popeye, Superman and other comic-strip characters, which he used in a window display at Bonwit Teller, a department store on Fifth Avenue. In 1962 he turned to the world of industrial design for his images – perhaps reflecting his earlier training at Carnegie Tech. *Big Campbell's Soup Can (19¢)*, which is among the earliest of these works, was painted in a scrupulously realistic style that the artist would soon abandon in favour of multiple compositions emphasizing the mass consumption of these commodities. Warhol also produced paintings of Coca-Cola bottles, dollar bills and stamps.

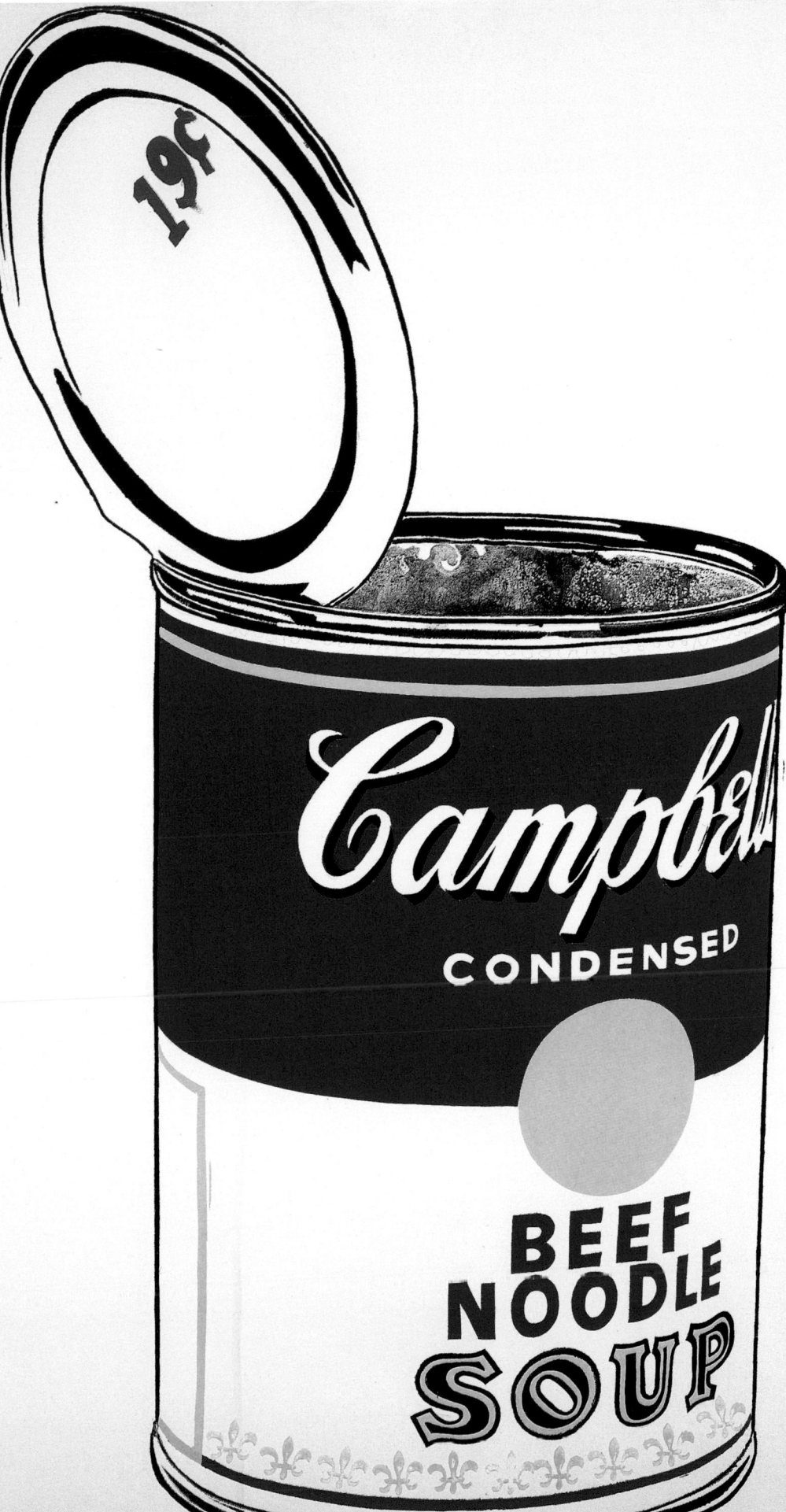

22

Patrick Caulfield (1936–)
Christ at Emmaus

1963. Oil on board, 101.1 x 127 cm. Royal College of Art, London

Patrick Caulfield was a member of the group of students at the Royal College of Art which included David Hockney, R.B. Kitaj and Peter Phillips. Caulfield, perhaps influenced by American Pop painters such as James Rosenquist and Roy Lichtenstein, favoured a cool, flat graphic style that interposed a wide emotional gulf between the artist and the viewer. Unlike other British Pop artists such as Paolozzi and Hamilton, who drew extensively upon American mass culture, Caulfield preferred to use images taken from art history. *Christ at Emmaus*, which was actually an assignment at the RCA, was based in part upon a painting by Delacroix (1798–1863). The palm-tree border, which seems to anticipate David Hockney's paintings of palm trees in Los Angeles, was borrowed from the design on a box of dried dates. The same year, Andy Warhol painted several canvases using the image of the *Mona Lisa* (Musée du Louvre, Paris), often in serial compositions with satirical titles such as *Thirty Are Better Than One* (Private collection); yet whereas Warhol is making a point of the banality of Leonardo's (1452–1519) massively over-reproduced portrait, Caulfield has a vital and altogether serious interest in the tradition of European easel painting. *Christ at Emmaus*, while unquestionably a work of Pop Art, quotes Delacroix in much the same way that Delacroix himself might have quoted a Renaissance master such as Michelangelo (1475–1564). The painting stands at the head of a long tradition of Pop paintings that borrow images from art history. Just before he died, Warhol produced an ambitious series of very large canvases based upon Leonardo's *Last Supper* (Fig. 23).

Fig. 23
Andy Warhol
The Last Supper
1986. Synthetic polymer
paint on canvas,
302.3 x 668 cm.
Museum of Modern Art,
New York

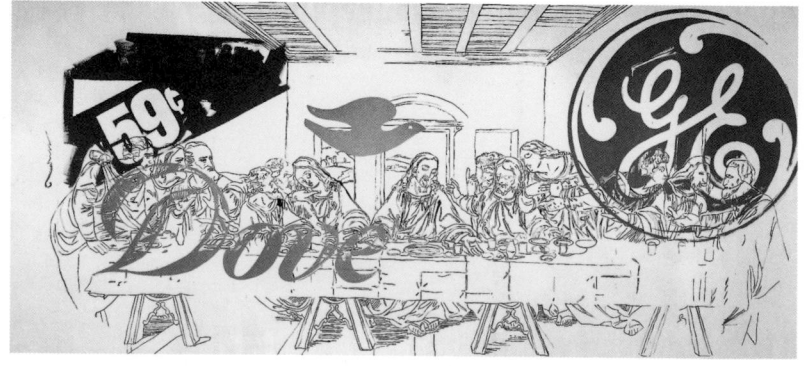

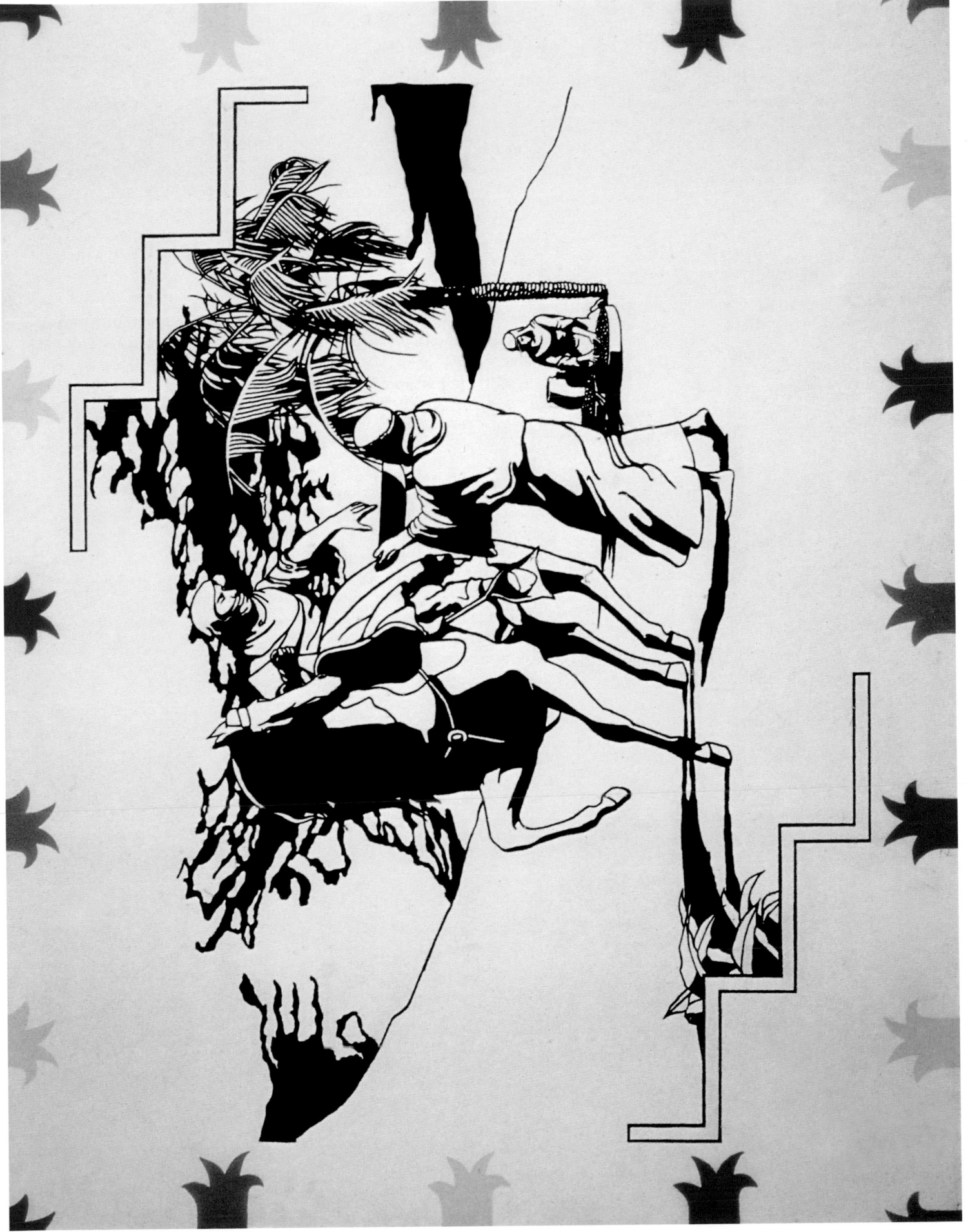

23

Robert Indiana (1928–)
The X-5

1963. Oil on canvas, 274.3 x 274.3 cm. Whitney Museum of American Art, New York

Many Pop artists used language in their works; as early as 1958 Jasper Johns painted the name 'Tennyson' across the bottom of one of his paintings, presenting a deliberate enigma which is perhaps esoteric in meaning. David Hockney, too, used quotations from Walt Whitman in his early Pop works in 1961. The American painter Robert Indiana used language much more explicitly, often to make political commentaries on the civil rights struggle in the American South and other issues of the day. Inevitably, these canvases now seem dated, and it is difficult to view them as anything but period pieces. Yet Indiana did paint what might well be the most familiar image to come out of Pop Art, the word 'LOVE', with a tilted O. The painting was the basis for innumerable posters, badges and other ephemera, as well as a U.S. postage stamp that remained popular for many years. Indiana's most successful works were a series based upon Charles Demuth's *I Saw the Figure 5 in Gold* (Fig. 20), which eight years before had served as the basis for Jasper Johns's *Figure 5*. Indiana found a personal numerological significance in the Demuth work, which was painted in the year of his birth. He painted *The X-5* in the year 1963, a number which, he said, 'when subtracted by 1928 leaves 35 – a number suggested by the succession of three fives (555) describing the sudden progression of the fire truck in the poet's existence.'

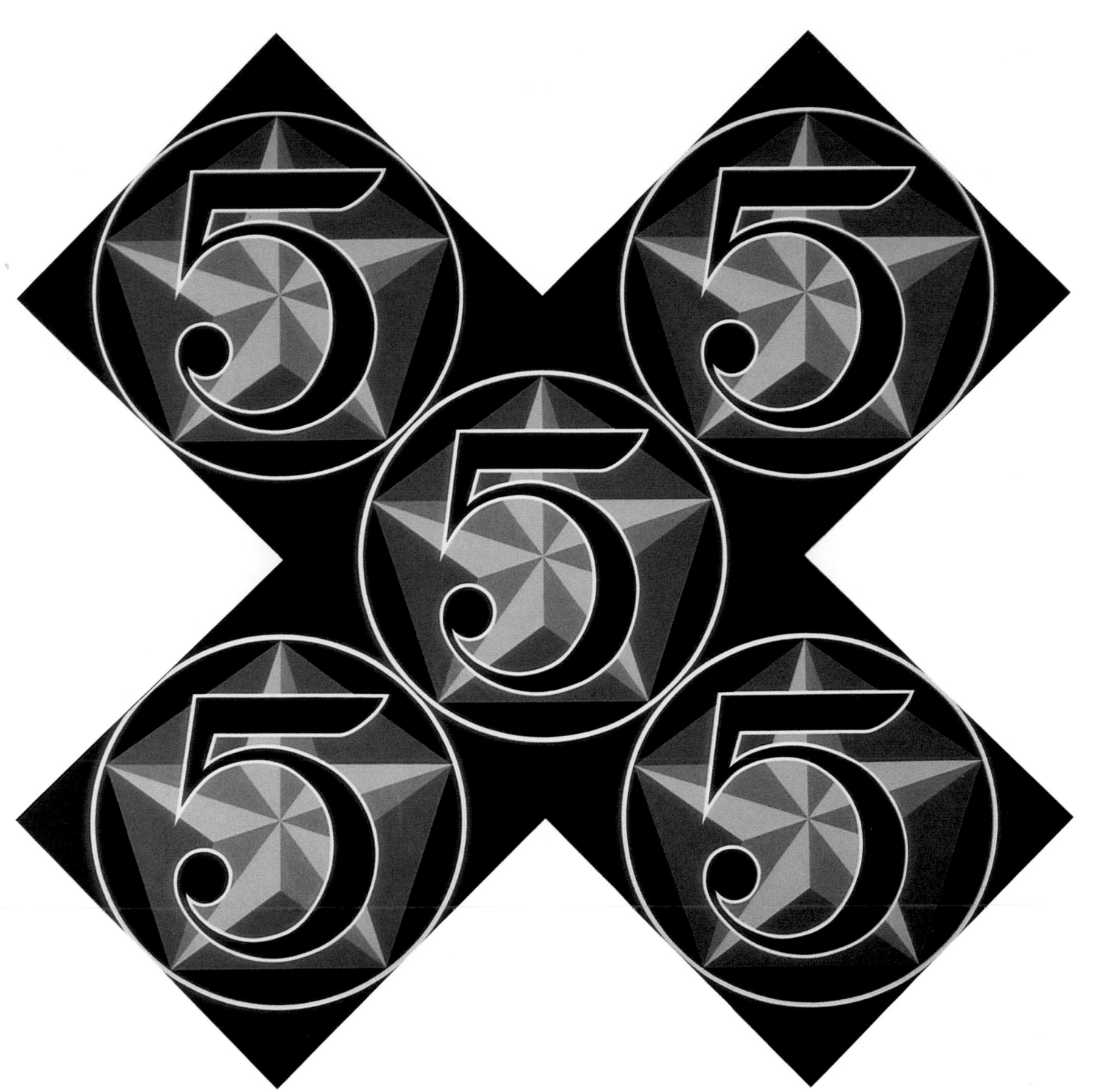

24

ROY LICHTENSTEIN (1923–)
Whaam!

1963. Oil and magna on canvas, 172.7 x 406.4 cm. Tate Gallery, London

Having found his mother lode of imagery in American comic books, Lichtenstein mined it sedulously and soon perfected his production methods. By 1963 his paintings had grown larger and more complex visually. This canvas, which measures more than four metres long (with a division into two panels), was about as large as any of the easel paintings being produced at that time. The result was overwhelming. Throughout the 1960s, American paintings grew ever larger; in 1965 Pop artist James Rosenquist created a multi-panel work called *F-111* (Private collection), which was 26 metres in length. Yet when it first appeared in 1963, *Whaam!* was one of the most impressive artworks, simply because of its size, that had ever been exhibited in America. It was revolutionary in other ways too: by incorporating the text of the comic strip, particularly the monumental onomatopoeic word that gives the work its title, Lichtenstein was flouting one of the canons of Western art. When earlier, 'traditional' artists such as Stuart Davis (see Fig. 10) had incorporated words into their designs, the intention had been naturalistic, to reflect language found in the landscape, such as a poster or a shop sign. Marcel Duchamp had also used words in some of his Dada works, but his blatant purpose was to thwart the viewer's expectations of what art should look like. Lichtenstein was even more subversive, transferring to his paintings found texts that had been plucked from the middle of a story unknown to the viewer. Yet it might be worth recalling that this is a device of epic poetry known as *in medias res*: epic poems typically begin 'in the middle'. The found texts in Lichtenstein's war-comic paintings seem at times to reflect, however dimly, the epic themes of glory and heroism found in Homer and Virgil.

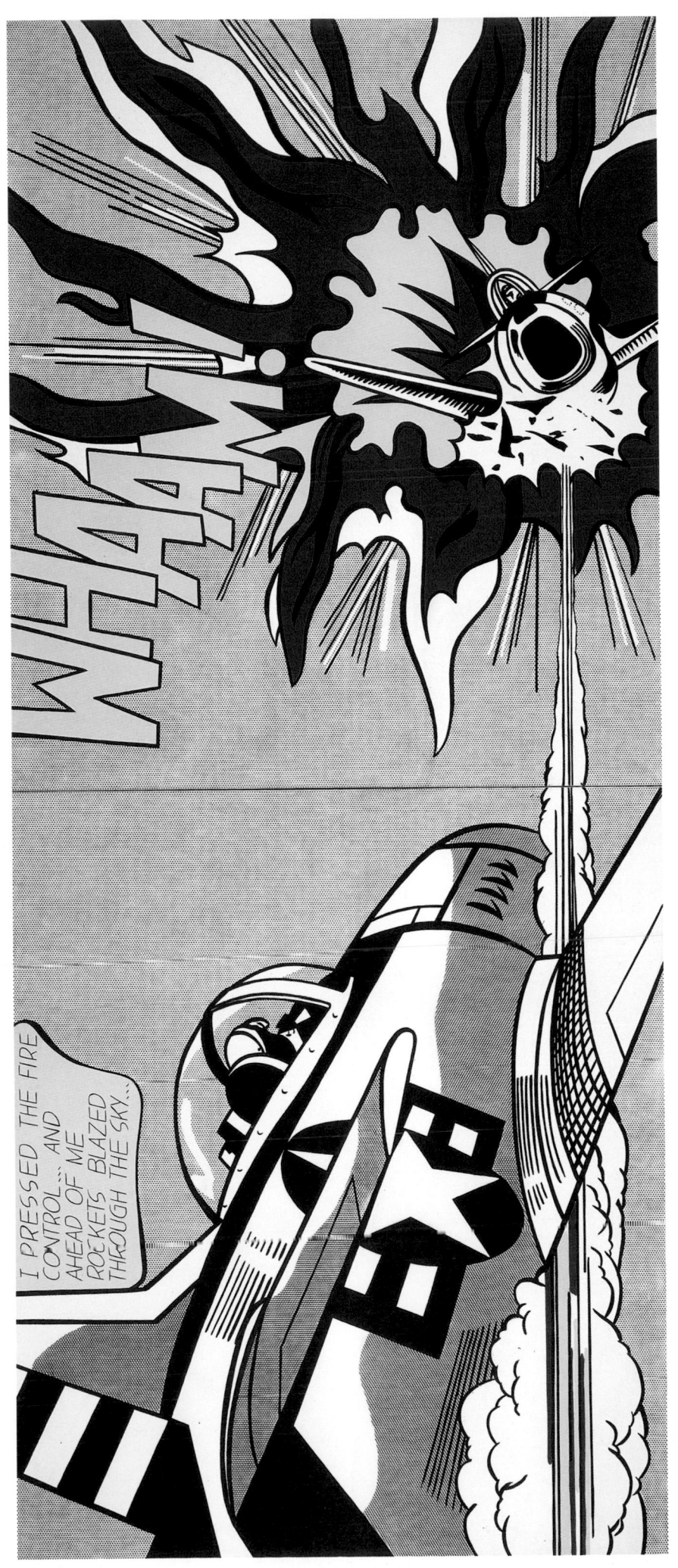

25

CLAES OLDENBURG (1929–)
Bedroom Ensemble

1963. Wood, vinyl, metal, fake fur, other materials, 518.2 x 640 cm. National Gallery of Canada, Ottawa

A Swedish immigrant living in the United States, sculptor Claes Oldenburg was rhapsodical about the vigour and freedom of life in America. He embraced the detritus of its mass consumer culture with an openness and an unalloyed delight that was unique among the Pop artists: the more lurid and tasteless the artefact, the closer it was to his heart. Yet Oldenburg also altered his images more profoundly than the other Pop artists, in ways that superficially seem to resemble the Abstract Expressionists. Whereas Rosenquist would routinely crop a found image, and Lichtenstein often simplified it slightly – and Warhol reproduced it photographically – Oldenburg produced lumpy, splashy, cartoon-like versions of objects in his sculpture. *Bedroom Ensemble* is the closest of any of his works to a 'straight' translation of his source. The British critic Lawrence Alloway, a founding member of the Independent Group (and, according to some sources, the man who gave Pop Art its name), describes the work: 'The *Bedroom Ensemble*, 1963, is a motel room, "apotheosized" (this is Oldenburg's word) in wood, formica, and vinyl. It has built-in perspective distortions that cause the bed to slant away from our own space, so that the initial impression of familiarity is warped … The room connotes both the fetishism and hygiene of American life, as well as the desolate calm that characterizes museum reconstructions of period rooms (and the *Ensemble* is always seen in either a gallery or a museum) … The *Bedroom Ensemble*, with its Marie Celeste-like suggestions of a recent presence in the purse and leopard-skin coat, is a monumental statement of the Pop art theme, human objects without the human body. The fact that it is a bedroom, the most intimate of living spaces, intensifies this effect.'

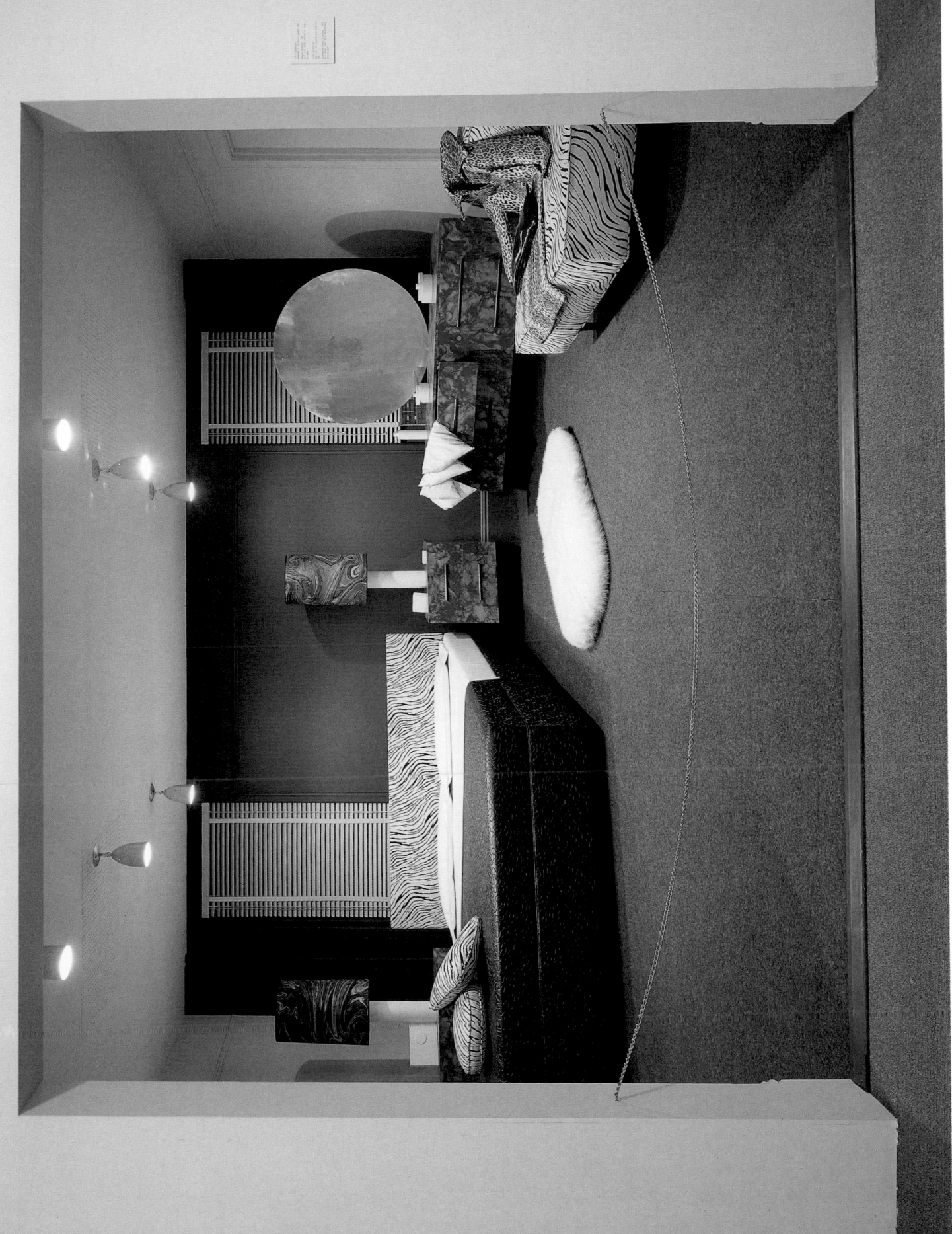

26

ED RUSCHA (1937–)
Noise

1963. Oil on canvas, 183 x 170.2 cm. Private collection

Painter Ed Ruscha was the unofficial leader of the Californian school of Pop Art. Ruscha came from his native Oklahoma to attend art school in Los Angeles, because, in Peter Plagens's phrase, of the city's 'abundance of hot-rod cars, street-level glamour, and cute girls'. In much the same way that the immigrant artist Claes Oldenburg embraced the exuberant vitality and colour of New York street life, Ruscha was attracted to the proverbial shallowness and rootlessness of California. He made his reputation as a painter with paintings of words and phrases in bold graphic designs. Like many Pop artists in New York, he had trained and worked as a commercial designer; in the 1960s he created the layouts for *Artforum* magazine, under the name Eddie Russia. In this work he is capitalizing on his commercial training by mimicking the loudness of noise with a loud graphic design. The enigmatic expanse of blue canvas is itself a sort of American, wide-open space. The work is rich with conceptual paradoxes; painting is the most silent of the arts, yet it can contain 'NOISE'.

Fig. 24
ED RUSCHA
Twentieth Century
Fox with Searchlights
1962. Oil on canvas, 169.5 x
338.5 cm. Whitney Museum
of American Art, New York

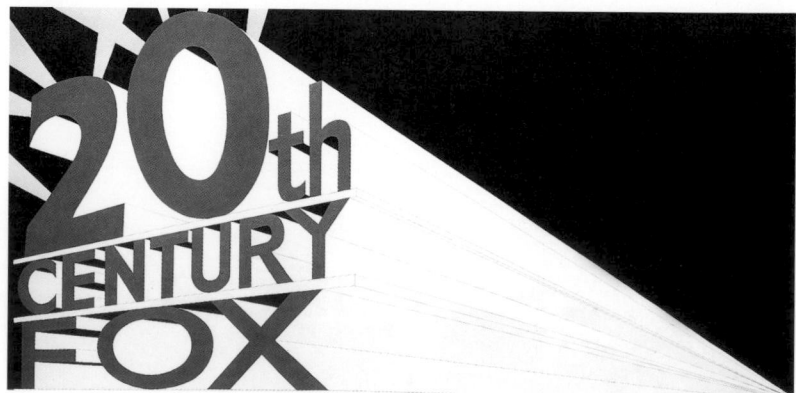

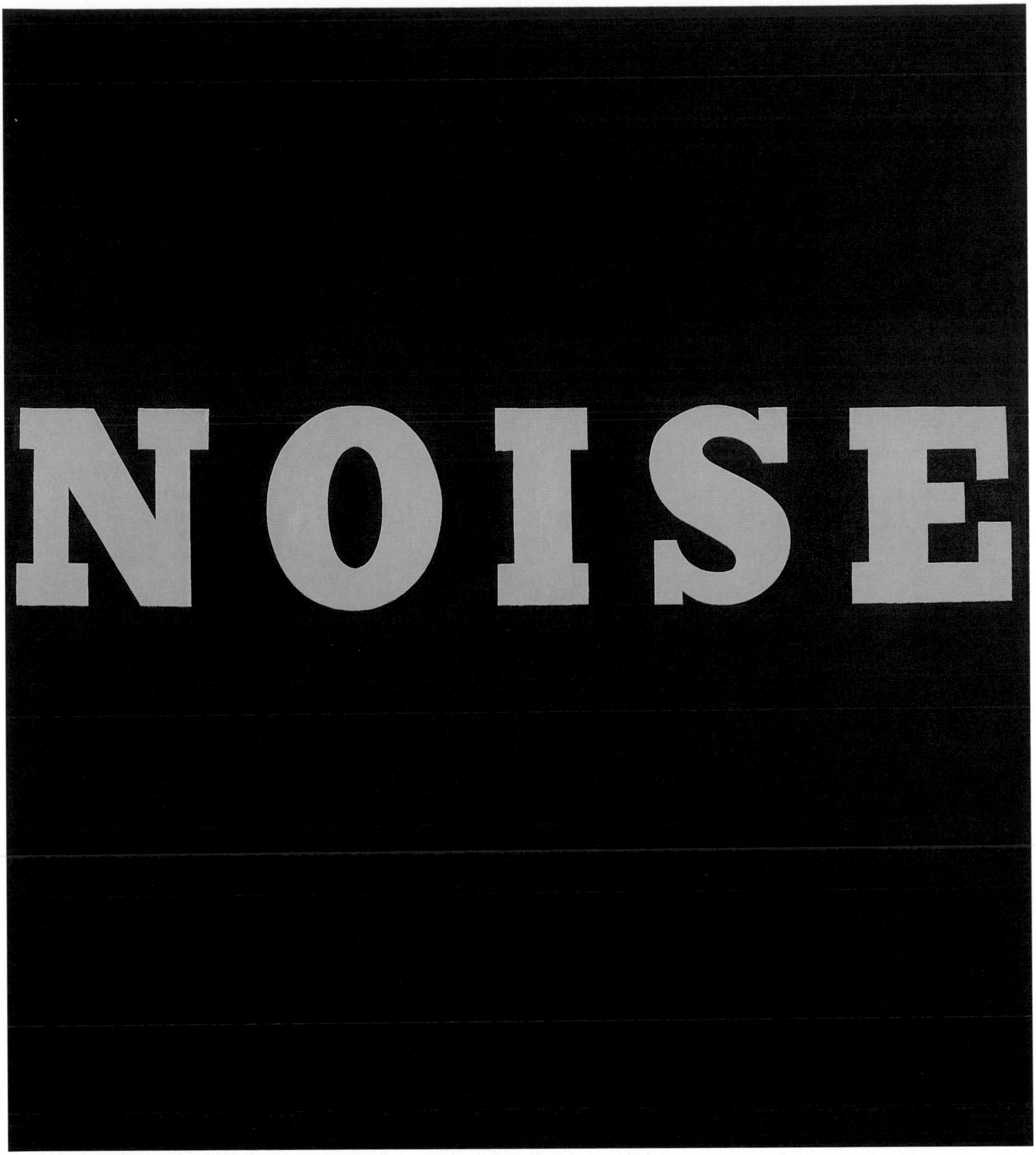
NOISE

27

George Segal (1924–)
The Gas Station

1963. Plaster and mixed media, 259.1 x 731.5 x 121.9 cm. National Gallery of Canada, Ottawa

The sculpture of George Segal fitted much more neatly within the context of Pop Art when it was known by one of its early names, the New Realism. His work has changed very little over many years: using live models, he creates monochromatic plaster casts of full figures, which are posed in settings containing mundane, frequently commercial, furnishings and objects. A native of New York, Segal's art addresses the issue of urban anonymity and isolation. While the mundane fixtures surrounding his figures echo the Pop idiom, particularly Tom Wesselmann's *Great American Nudes* (Plate 29), his sculptures have a direct emotional appeal which is at odds with the cool sensibility of most American Pop artists. His figures, always left unfinished and ghostly white, seem insubstantial in the context of the real objects that make up their environment. Segal's use of life casts in some ways resembles Robert Rauschenberg's and Andy Warhol's use of the silkscreen, as a way of lifting images directly from 'life', but the human individuality of his figures gives them a poignancy and emotional urgency akin to the life- and death-masks common in the nineteenth century, and even suggests the casts of the victims of the eruption of Mt. Vesuvius at Pompeii. In his latter career, Segal has frequently been commissioned to create public sculpture, such as a controversial group in New York's Sheridan Square, which celebrates the gay liberation movement.

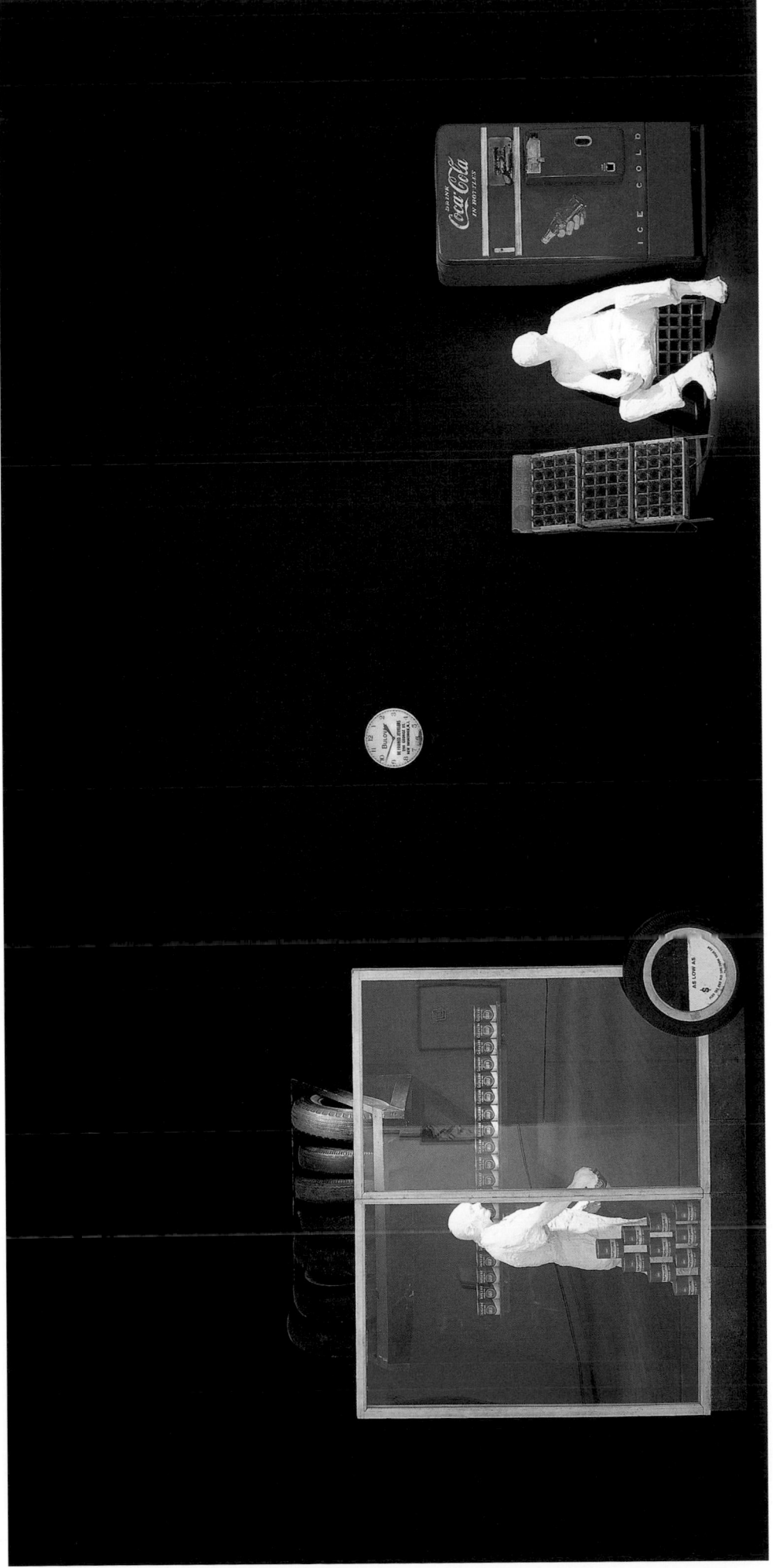

28

ANDY WARHOL (1928–86)
Red Race Riot

1963. Silkscreen ink on synthetic polymer paint on canvas, 350 x 210 cm. Museum Ludwig, Cologne

His reputation (or at least his fame) having been secured by paintings of commercial products and celebrities, in 1963 Andy Warhol began a series he called the Disasters, which were among the most powerful and controversial works he ever produced. These paintings are based on horrific newspaper photographs of violent or macabre aspects of American life: gory images of car crashes, a suicide's leap, a gangster's funeral, a page from a newspaper describing the deaths of people who had eaten tuna fish from a contaminated tin. This serial composition is taken from a photograph of an infamous race riot in the South. The composition appears to be completely unpremeditated; each of the screened images was laid down randomly, with no discernible design motive, until there was no longer room for any more.

This mindless repetitiveness has the effect of deflating the disturbing content of the image. Although Warhol claimed that he did not have an editorial message in the Disaster series, there can be little doubt that by treating the most awful aspects of contemporary American life in exactly the same way as he treated inoffensive banalities such as soup cans, he was at least implying that race riots and car crashes had become commonplaces in American society. These paintings are shocking not only in their content but also visually: the superimposed images vibrate optically over the intense background colours, an effect similar to that of a short-lived art movement of the 1960s called Op Art, which relied entirely upon creating vertiginous optical effects.

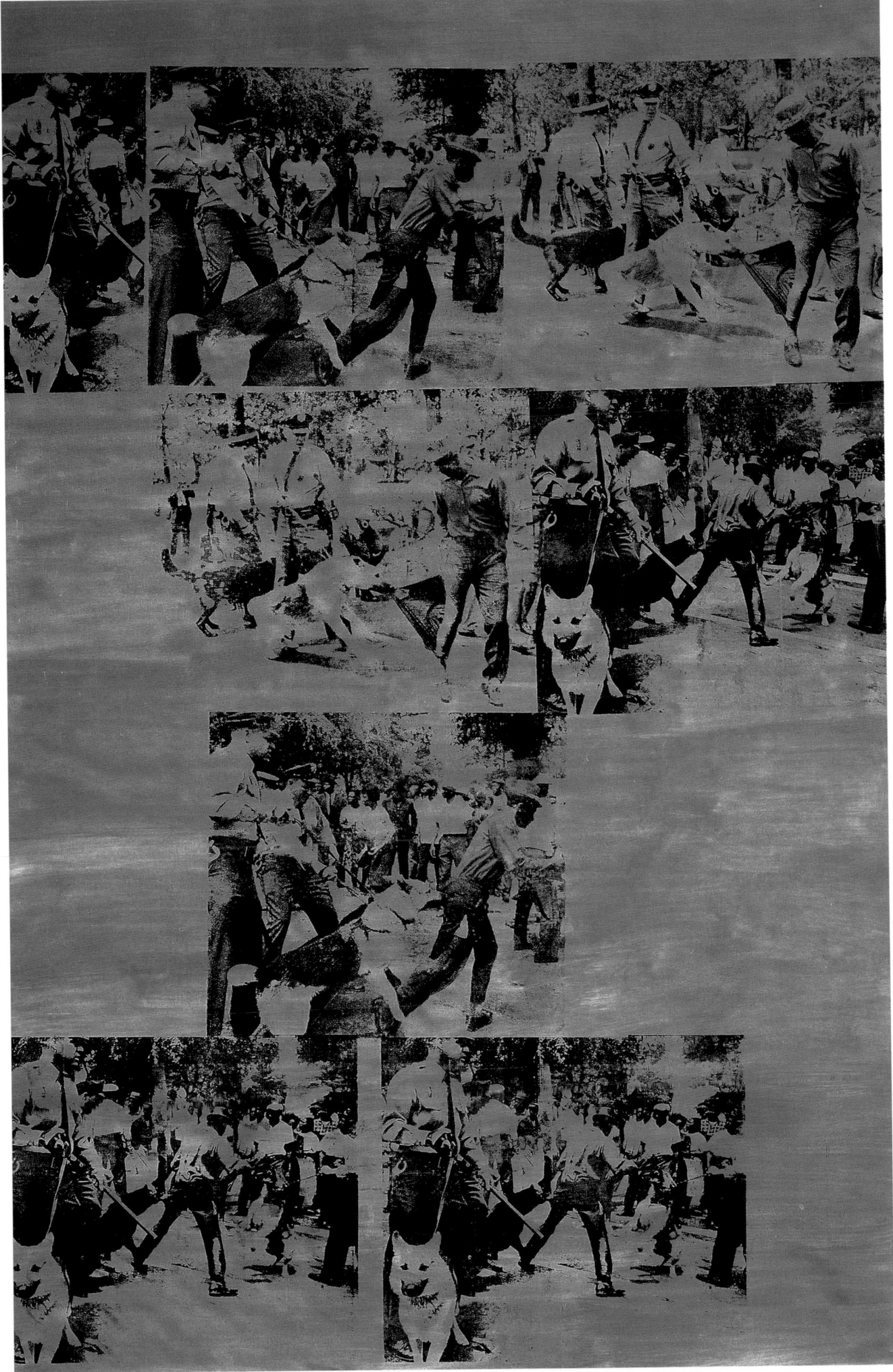

29

TOM WESSELMANN (1931–)
Bathtub Nude Number 3

1963. Mixed media, 213.4 x 269.2 x 45.1 cm. Museum Ludwig, Cologne

One frequently noted peculiarity of Pop Art is the fact that, while it is concerned with the life and environment of the average person in contemporary urban society, average people are themselves only rarely encountered. And when human figures are present, they tend to be flattened and dehumanized: in Warhol's paintings they are rendered as fuzzy, photographic icons, in Lichtenstein's they are brainless caricatures, and in Segal's sculptures they are transformed into lost, zombie-like figures. This dehumanizing process is most acutely present in the work of Tom Wesselmann, whose mixed-media works present scrupulously real settings for transparently fake human figures. Wesselmann took Rauschenberg's concept of the combine painting and tidied it up, removing the element of funk which, paradoxically, was largely responsible for the elegance of Rauschenberg's works. Wesselmann created banal, hygienic fragments of domestic American architecture, which housed flat, anti-illusionistic female nudes. Wesselmann's women were, in Lawrence Alloway's words, 'blank schemata animated only at the erogenous zones of mouth, nipple, and groin.' When Wesselmann's pseudo-pornography was first exhibited, it was considered to be very sophisticated, and to arise from a cool attitude of detachment and indifference; changes in sexual politics, however, have left Wesselmann's nudes looking naive and dated.

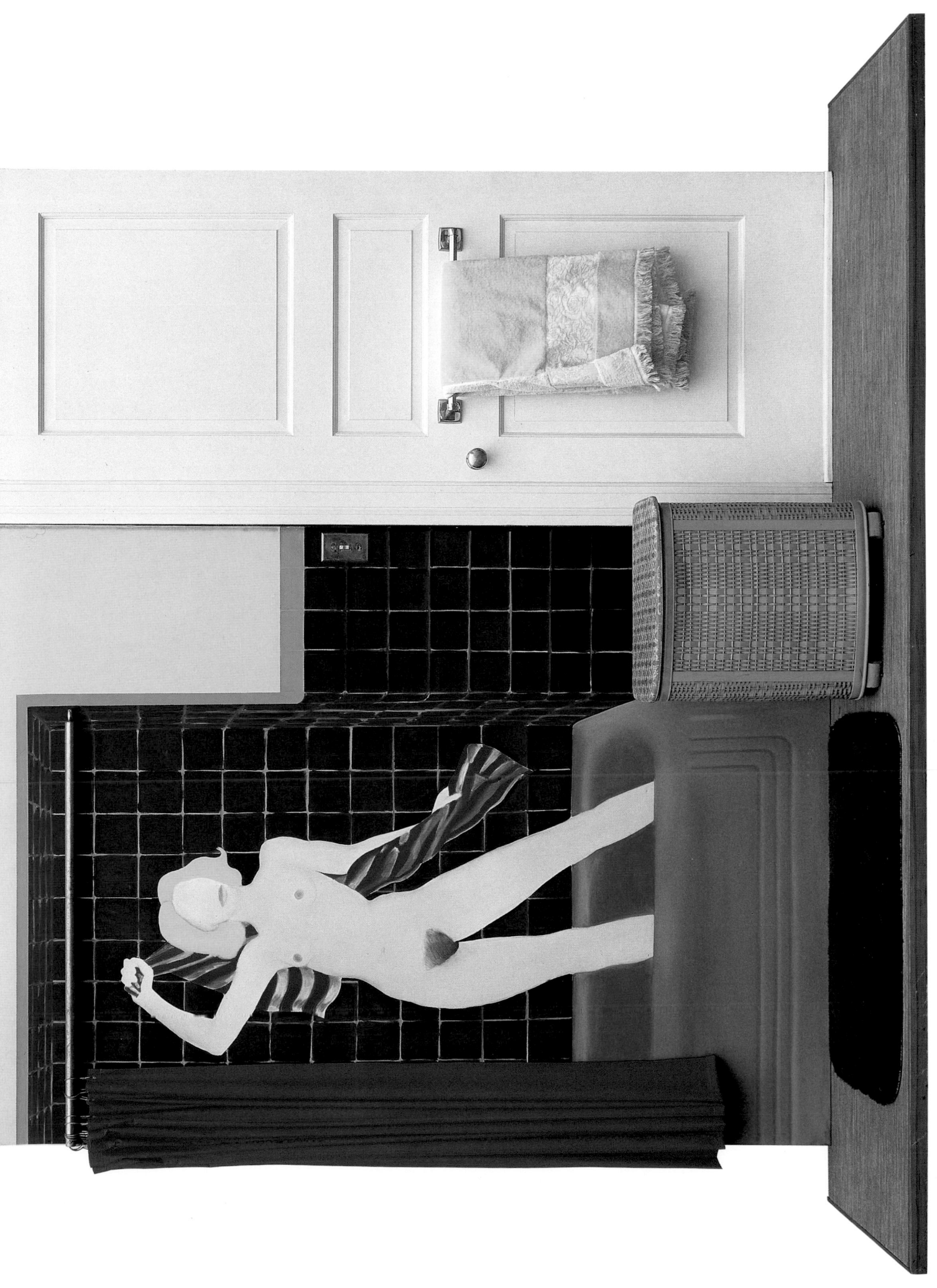

30

RICHARD HAMILTON (1922–)
Interior II

1964. Oil, collage, metal relief, cellulose on panel, 121.9 x 162.6 cm. Tate Gallery, London

In his mature work, Hamilton was profoundly influenced by the American Pop artists. The dominant image in *Interior II* is an altered still photograph of an American actress. While the American Pop artists tended to use images of famous pop personalities, Hamilton has chosen a very obscure actress named Patricia Knight. (The image was taken from a 1949 Hollywood cop movie called *Shockproof*, directed by Douglas Sirk.) The mood of Hamilton's painting manages to be at once celebratory of the culture that produced the *film noir* and also to convey something of its forbidding atmosphere. Hamilton's career began with the collage *Just What Is It That Makes Today's Homes So Different, So Appealing?* (Plate 7), and he continued to use collage elements extensively throughout his career: here, elements of the architecture are created by the use of Fablon, a plastic veneer used for refinishing cupboards; to the left of the figure is a small piece of real mirror, which, according to the critic Marco Livingstone, 'serves to incorporate the space in which we are standing into that of the picture and to suggest that we are also willingly colluding in whatever sinister event is about to take place.'

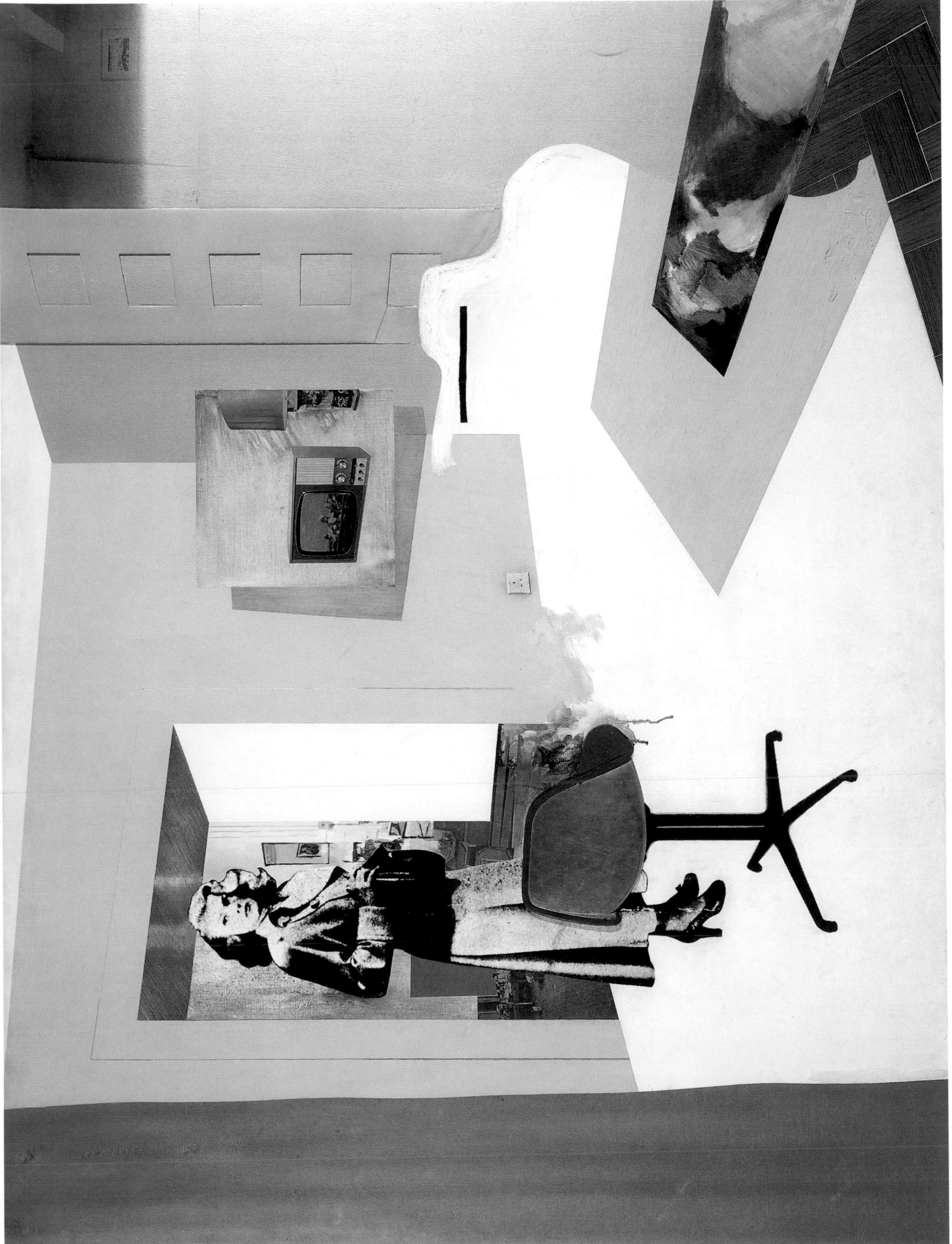

31

MARISOL (1930–)
Women and Dog

1964. Mixed media, 182.9 x 208.3 x 40.6 cm. Whitney Museum of American Art, New York

Born in Paris of Venezuelan parents, Escobar Marisol grew up in Paris and Los Angeles, and in 1950 came to New York, where she studied at the Art Students League and the Hans Hofmann School. She began to work as a sculptor in wood, and was soon adding painted and photographic images, plaster and metal elements, and found objects. Most of her works are mordantly satirical human figures, such as this group of shoppers. The three-faced female figures are not only an affectionate parody of Cubist works but there is also the suggestion that the women are changeable and shallow – much worse than two-faced. Many of Marisol's works have strong associations with commercial American folk sculpture and are reminiscent of the nineteenth-century cigar-store Indian. The carving is always deliberately crude, in contrast to the sophistication of much of the imagery. While Marisol has made a number of works that are self-consciously in the Pop idiom – a famous multimedia Coca-Cola bottle, for example, and a portrait of Andy Warhol – her work has a deadpan irony verging on whimsy, and a handmade 'artsy-craftsiness' that sets her well outside the mainstream of the movement.

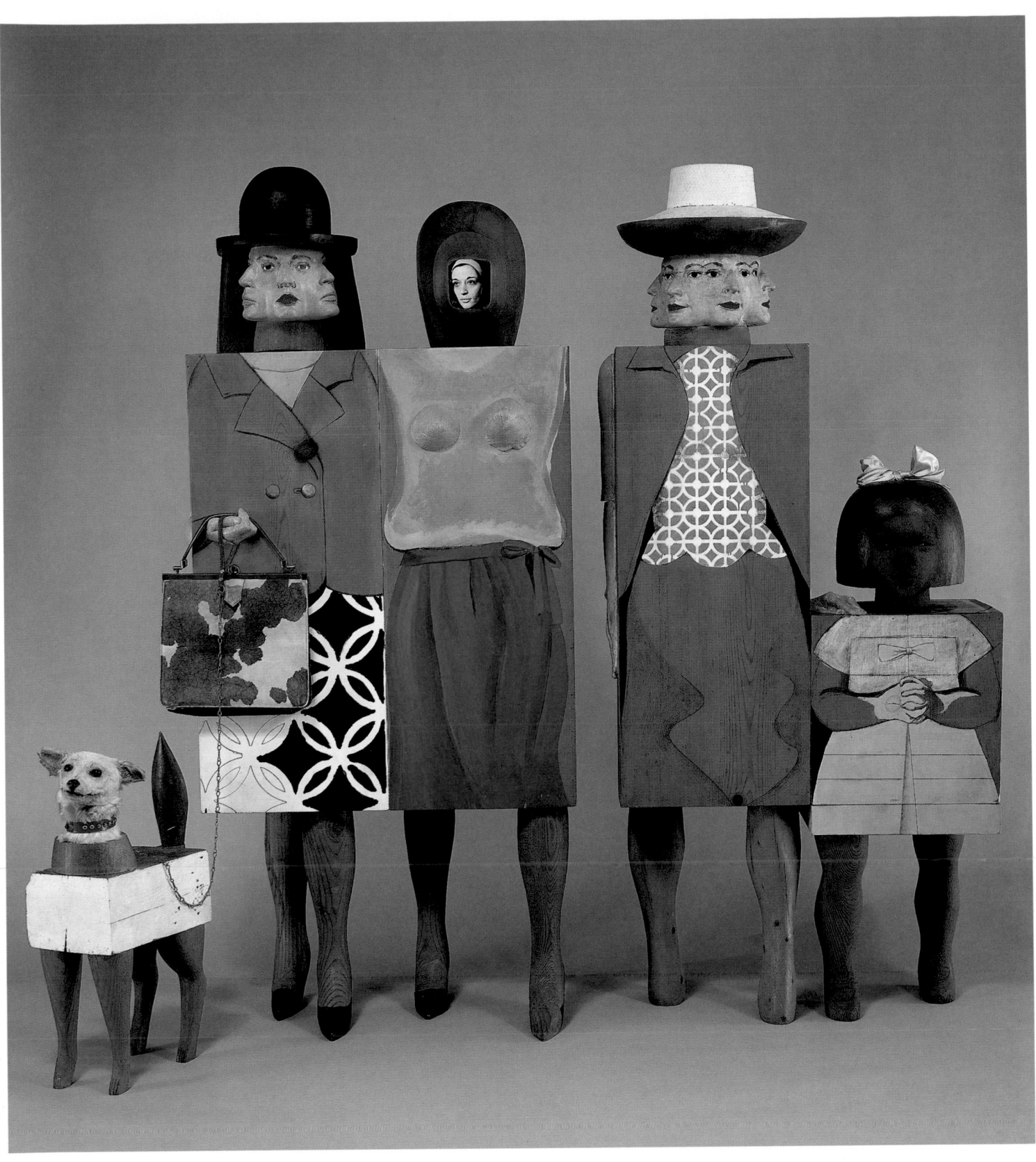

32

ROBERT RAUSCHENBERG (1925–)
Persimmon

1964. Oil on canvas with silkscreen, 167.6 x 127 cm. Private collection

In his later work, Rauschenberg was influenced by his own creative progeny, particularly Andy Warhol, who introduced the use of silk-screened photographic images into his paintings. The central image here is a silkscreen of Rubens's *Venus at her Toilet*, which is one of the very few quotations from art history in Rauschenberg's whole career. The differences in the way the two artists use the silkscreened image reflect the defiant anti-art gestures of the earliest Pop artists of the 1950s, and the cooler approach of the 1960s. Rauschenberg has applied the silkscreen with a deliberate messiness, and the composition is crowded and jumbled, giving an overall impression of funkiness that relates the painting directly to the combines of his earlier career. Warhol, by contrast, tended either to design his paintings as neatly as possible, as in *Marilyn* (Plate 34), or to lay the images down randomly but with a great deal of 'breathing space', as in *Red Race Riot* (Plate 28). The crowded New York City street scene at the top of this painting also reflects a growing interest in the city itself, which had been inspired by Claes Oldenburg, among others. The early works of Johns and Rauschenberg were deliberately non-specific in their references, and could have been created anywhere.

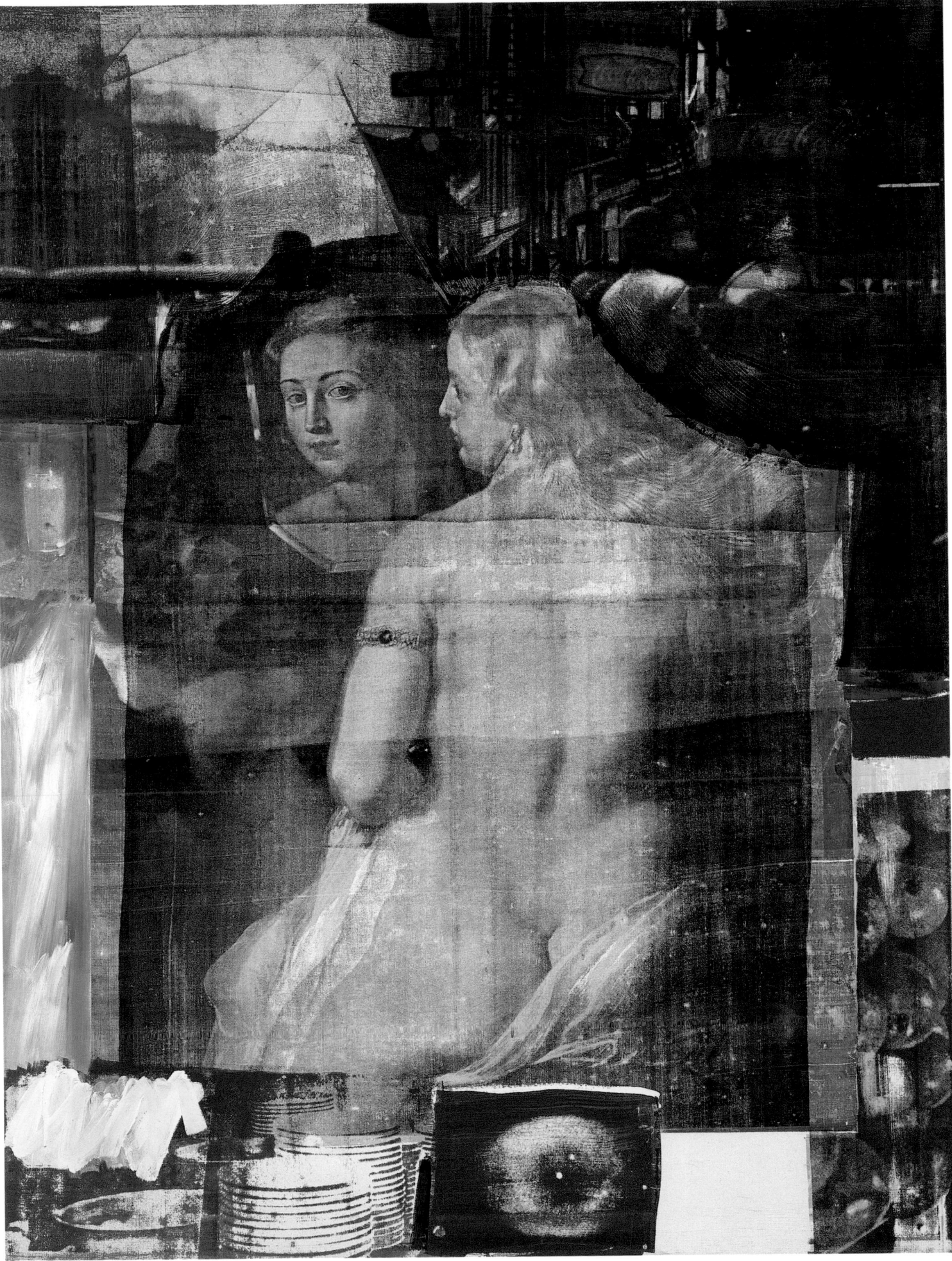

33 JAMES ROSENQUIST (1933–)
Untitled, Joan Crawford Says

1964. Oil on canvas, 233.7 x 198.1 cm. Museum Ludwig, Cologne

Rosenquist's paintings employ many graphic artifices to emphasize the continuity between the canvas and life. The radical cropping of images, as in this detail from a magazine advertisement for cigarettes, implies that the image continues beyond the picture frame into the space occupied by the viewer – a device frequently used by Degas in his scenes of the racetrack and of ballet dancers. This painting is somewhat unusual in Rosenquist's œuvre, in that its image is borrowed directly from a single source, rather than being a jumble of images from disparate sources: it could stand alone as a section of a billboard poster. The image of movie star Joan Crawford is enigmatic. On the one hand she has the bizarre, almost monumental appearance that would later make her one of the figures from American pop culture most beloved of the 'camp' sensibility; but at the same time the artist's portrayal, flat though it is, evinces a certain sympathy and sincerity. In some respects James Rosenquist was the purest of Pop artists, for his own creative role was purely graphic, and all his paintings are unique expressions of images from popular culture.

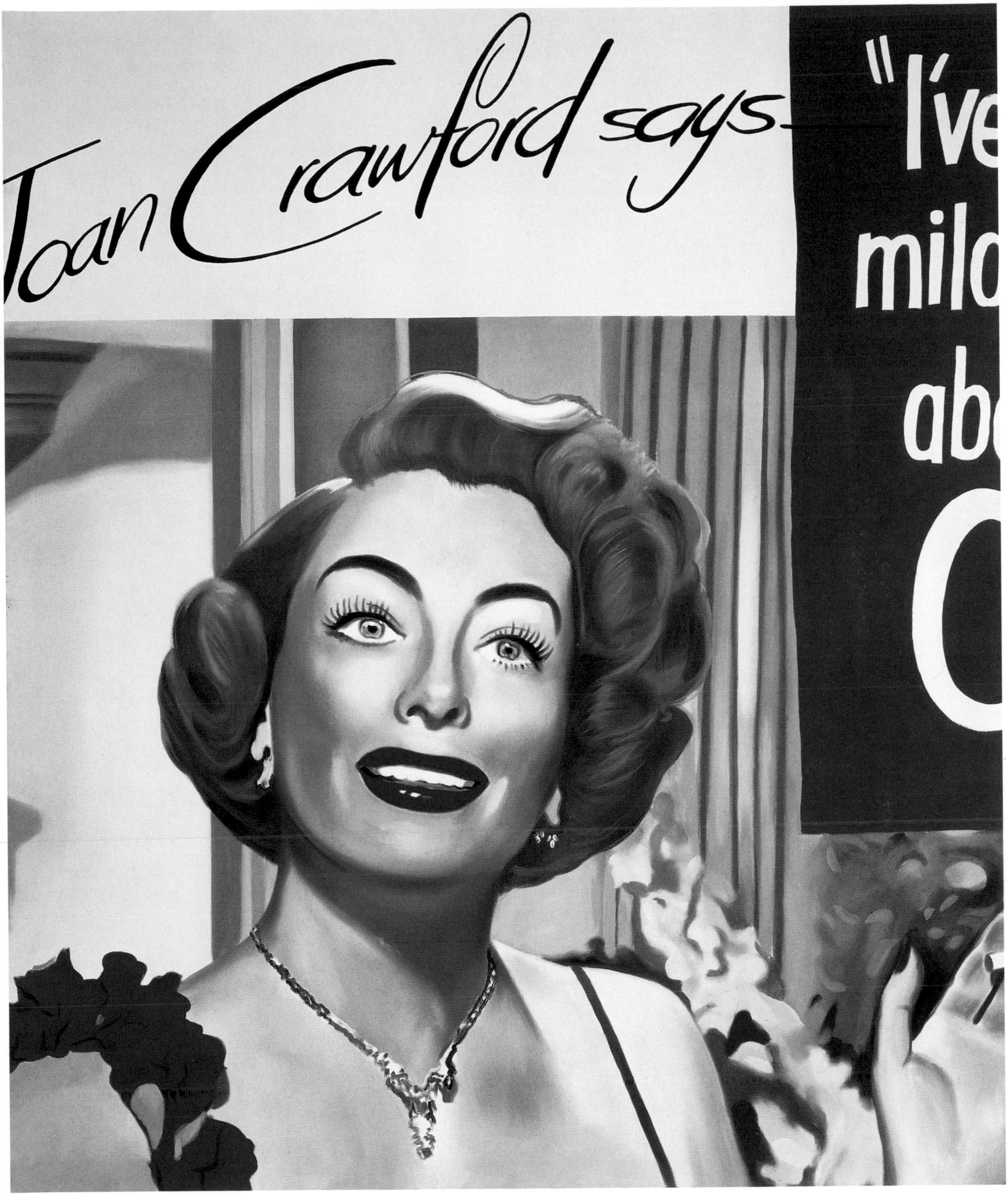
Joan Crawford says–
"I've
milo
abo
C

Andy Warhol (1928–86)
Marilyn

1967. Serigraph, printed in colour composition, 91.5 x 91.5 cm. Museum of Modern Art, New York

At the same time as he was producing paintings of commercial products, Warhol began his famous series of movie stars and other famous people. Marilyn Monroe, Jacqueline Kennedy and Elvis Presley were the subject of many large canvases, as were minor personalities such as Troy Donahue and Natalie Wood. Although he always denied that he was creating a social commentary in his art, it is safe to assume that the artist was making a conceptual equivalence between a celebrity such as Marilyn Monroe and commercial products such as a can of soup or a bottle of Coca-Cola: all of them might be properly described as corporate creations, disposable commodities intended for mass consumption. These paintings were produced by using silkscreens made from found photographic images, which were laid directly onto the canvas and printed with synthetic polymer paint.

In many paintings in his Marilyn Monroe and Elizabeth Taylor series, Warhol used different screens for the hair, lips and eyes, laying down intense shades of primary colours – in the case of Marilyn Monroe, for example, yellow hair, aquamarine eyes and red lips – in lurid parody of the actresses' highly exaggerated expression of feminine beauty. In 1963 he made serial paintings of Elizabeth Taylor in her cleavage-baring costume for the title role of Joseph L. Mankiewicz's film *Cleopatra*, one of the most spectacular flops in Hollywood history. The following year came a series of paintings of Marilyn Monroe's lips, floating menacingly on the canvas in serried ranks. In these paintings, Warhol pushed far beyond his stated aim of merely reflecting the culture going on around him, creating works that approached conventional satire.

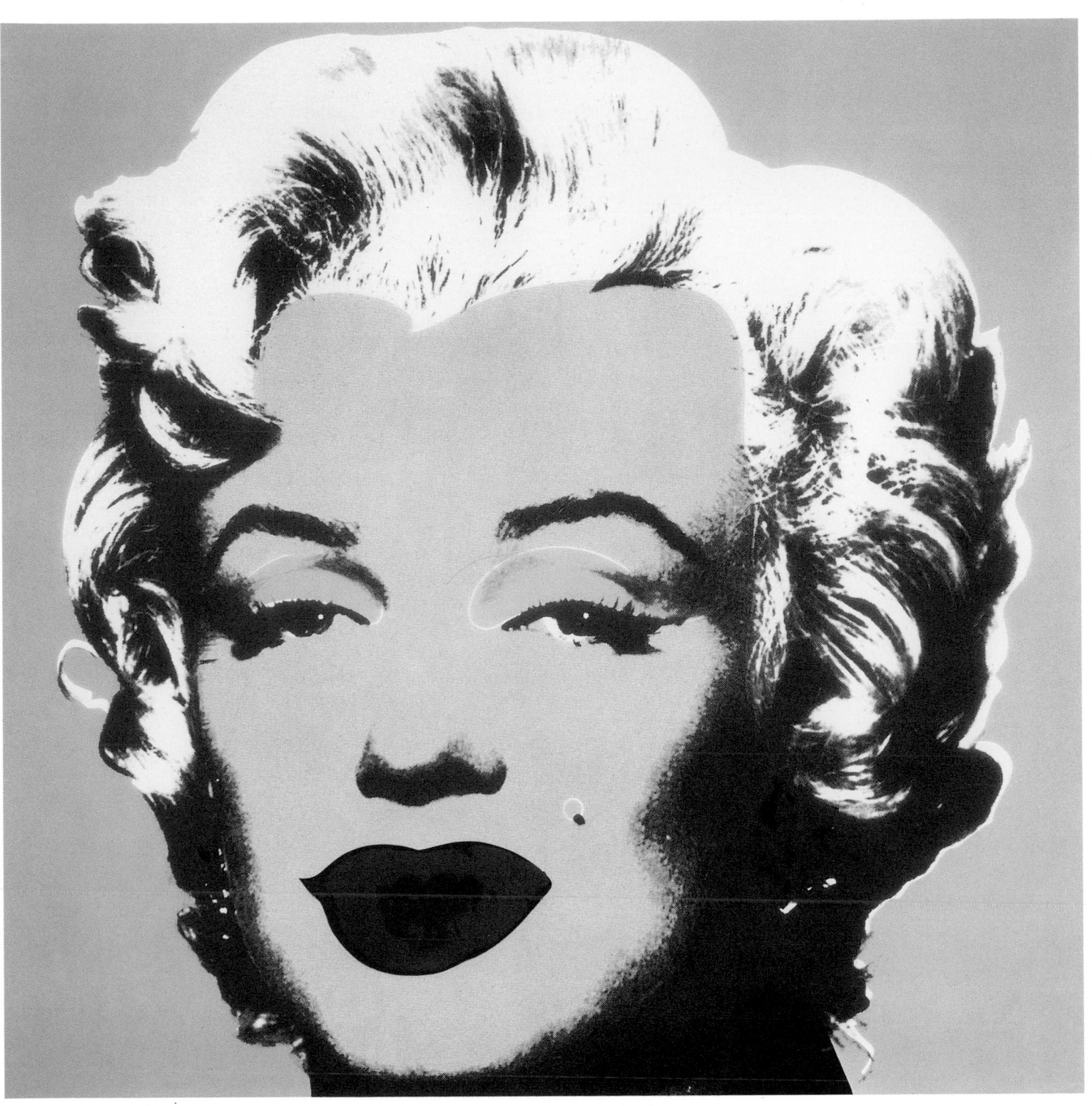

35

EDUARDO PAOLOZZI (1924–)
Wittgenstein in New York

1965. Screen-print, 96 x 66 cm. Scottish National Gallery of Modern Art, Edinburgh

Paolozzi's mature works are characterized by a mechanistic, brightly colourful graphic style. His most coherent statement in the Pop idiom was a portfolio called *As Is When* (1965), which was based on the life and works of the Austrian-born English philosopher Ludwig Wittgenstein. Wittgenstein was a powerful influence on several American Pop pioneers, particularly Jasper Johns, who found in his writings licence to liberate art from its need to have 'something to say'; the existence of the object was in itself the only meaningful statement art can make. Paolozzi, like Johns and Robert Rauschenberg, gloried in the ordinary, and incorporated absolutely any kind of visual imagery in his work, from scientific and industrial diagrams to banal advertisements. Like the Kentish Pop artist Peter Blake, Paolozzi was himself tremendously influential in the popular media; his brilliantly coloured posters were a fixture of the graphic scene in Britain in the 1960s.

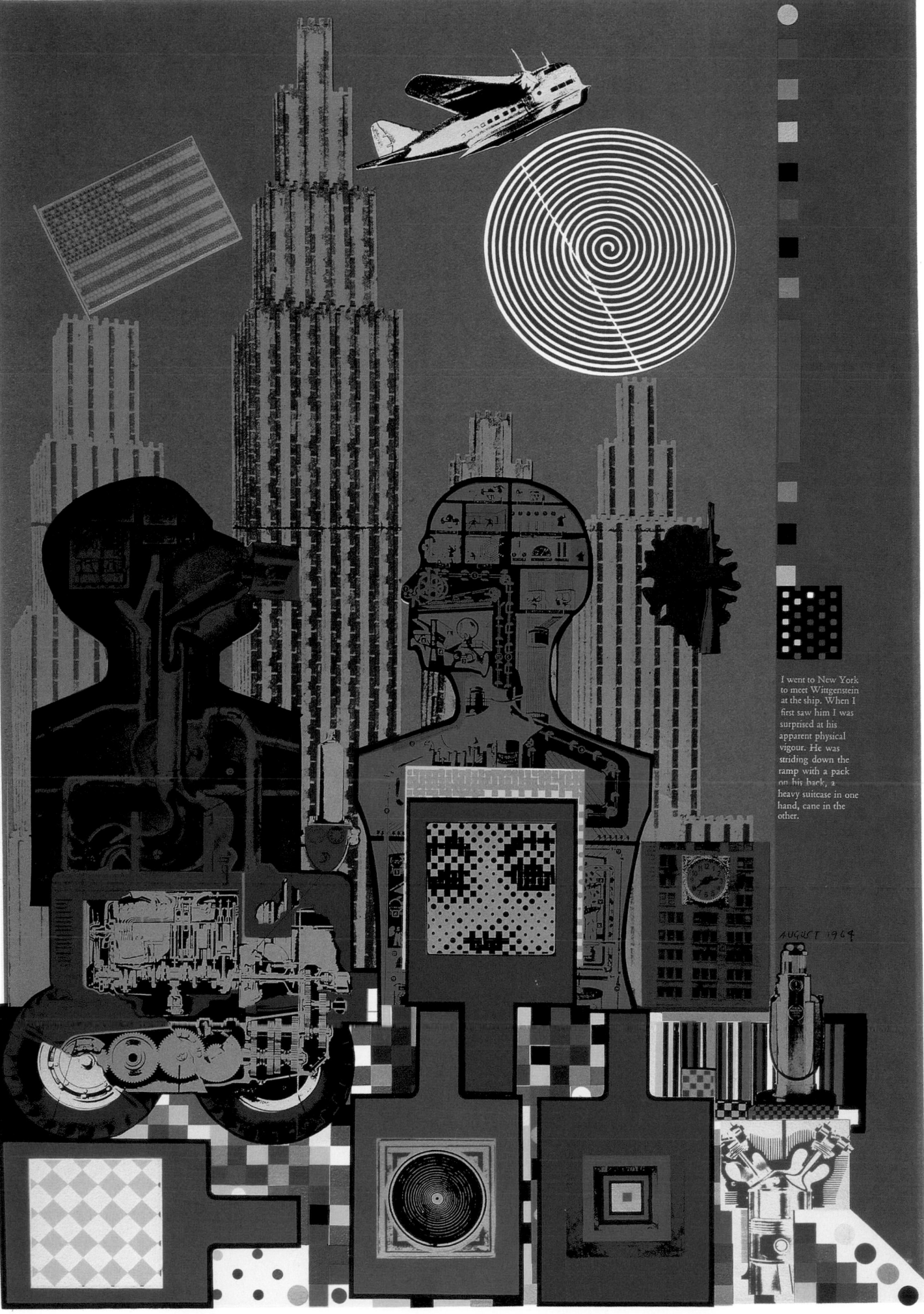

I went to New York
to meet Wittgenstein
at the ship. When I
first saw him I was
surprised at his
apparent physical
vigour. He was
striding down the
ramp with a pack
on his back, a
heavy suitcase in one
hand, cane in the
other.

AUGUST 1964

36

MEL RAMOS (1935–)
Micronite Mary

1965. Oil on canvas, 177.8 x 155 cm. Private collection

Early in his career, the Californian painter Mel Ramos was deeply influenced by Wayne Thiebaud (see Plate 8), who was producing images of Pop icons that were at once creamily painterly and yet emotionally neutral. Ramos was one of the first American artists to paint characters from comic books, notably a series of monumental portraits of Superman and Batman that date to 1961. Ramos then shifted to another source of 'junk' imagery: girlie magazines. He put together glossy images of brainless, compliant women with consumer products in arbitrary combinations reminiscent of James Rosenquist's poster paintings. *Micronite Mary* clearly suggests that the naked woman is a product to be picked up, used and tossed aside, like a cigarette. (The painting's title refers to a patented ingredient of the filter of this particular brand of cigarettes.) Ramos outrageously pushed the limits of acceptable taste beyond what most people in the art world at that time were prepared for. These semi-pornographic paintings flouted the conventions not only of 'straight', 'square' society but also those of the intelligentsia. By presenting women in degrading circumstances at a time when the women's rights movement was gaining strength in the United States, Ramos challenged the very legitimacy of the canons of good taste, anticipating the deliberate vulgarity of later artists such as Jeff Koons (see Plate 47).

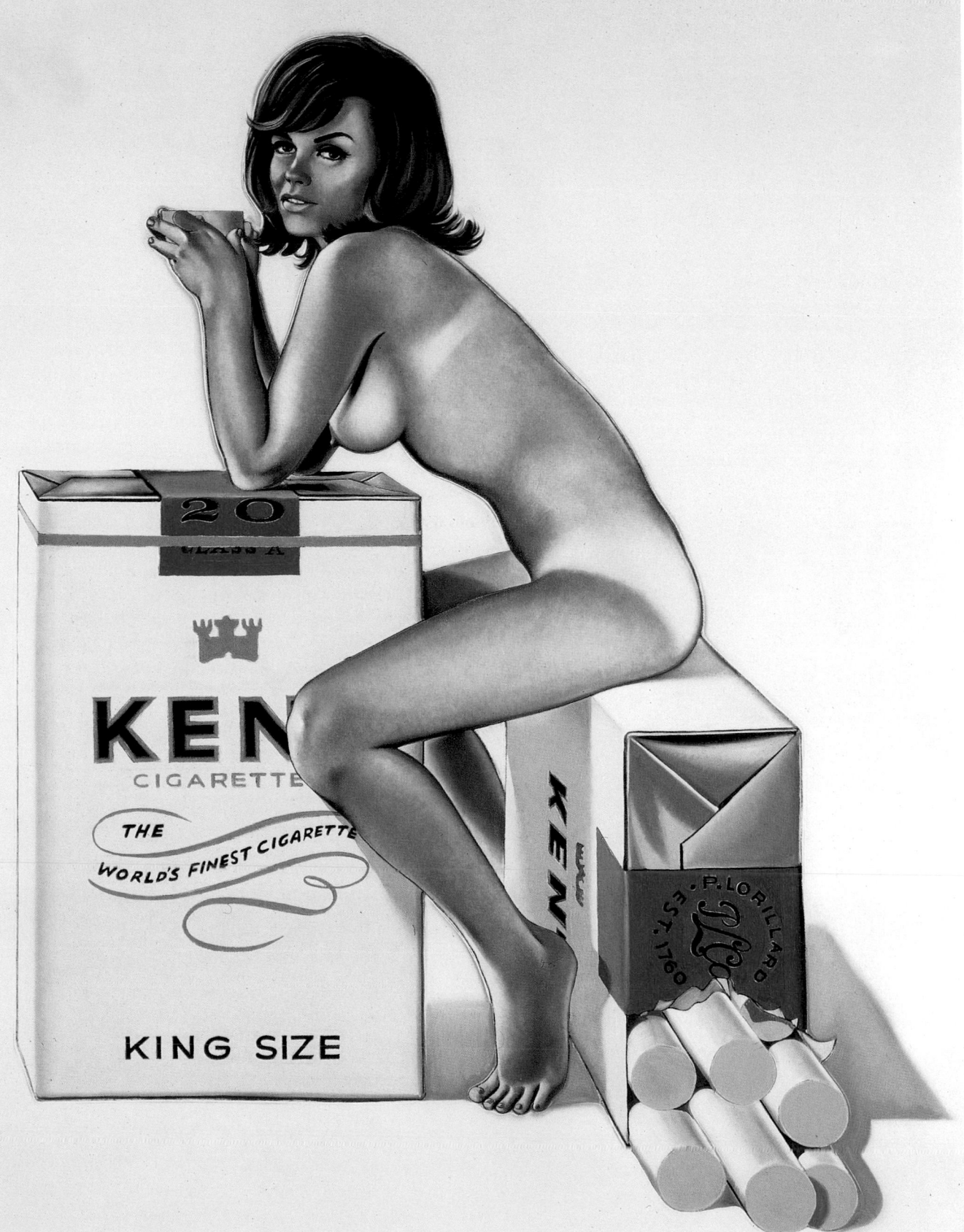

37

PETER PHILLIPS (1939–)
Custom Painting No. 5

1965. Acrylic on canvas, 172 x 300 cm. Galerie Bischofberger, Zürich

A classmate of Caulfield, Hockney and Kitaj at the Royal College of Art in the late 1950s, Peter Phillips was, of all the British Pop artists, the most openly approving of the mass culture, primarily American, that supplied his art with its images. He lived in America from 1964 to 1967 and there he found strong support for his love of the flashy, slick culture of the streets. Early in his career, Phillips decided not to transform found images in his art, reasoning, in Marco Livingstone's words, that 'whatever had stimulated his imagination could operate in a similar way for the spectator if integrated into painting in the same form'. Yet it would be an error to confuse Phillips's aesthetic with that of Duchamp in his famous readymades (see Fig. 8), for Phillips is a fervent believer in the power of the painted image. Executed with an airbrush in almost blindingly brilliant colours, Phillips's canvases have a highly finished, glossy appearance that is even more viscerally powerful than his sources. In the 'flesh', paintings such as *Custom Painting No. 5* dazzle and ravish the eye.

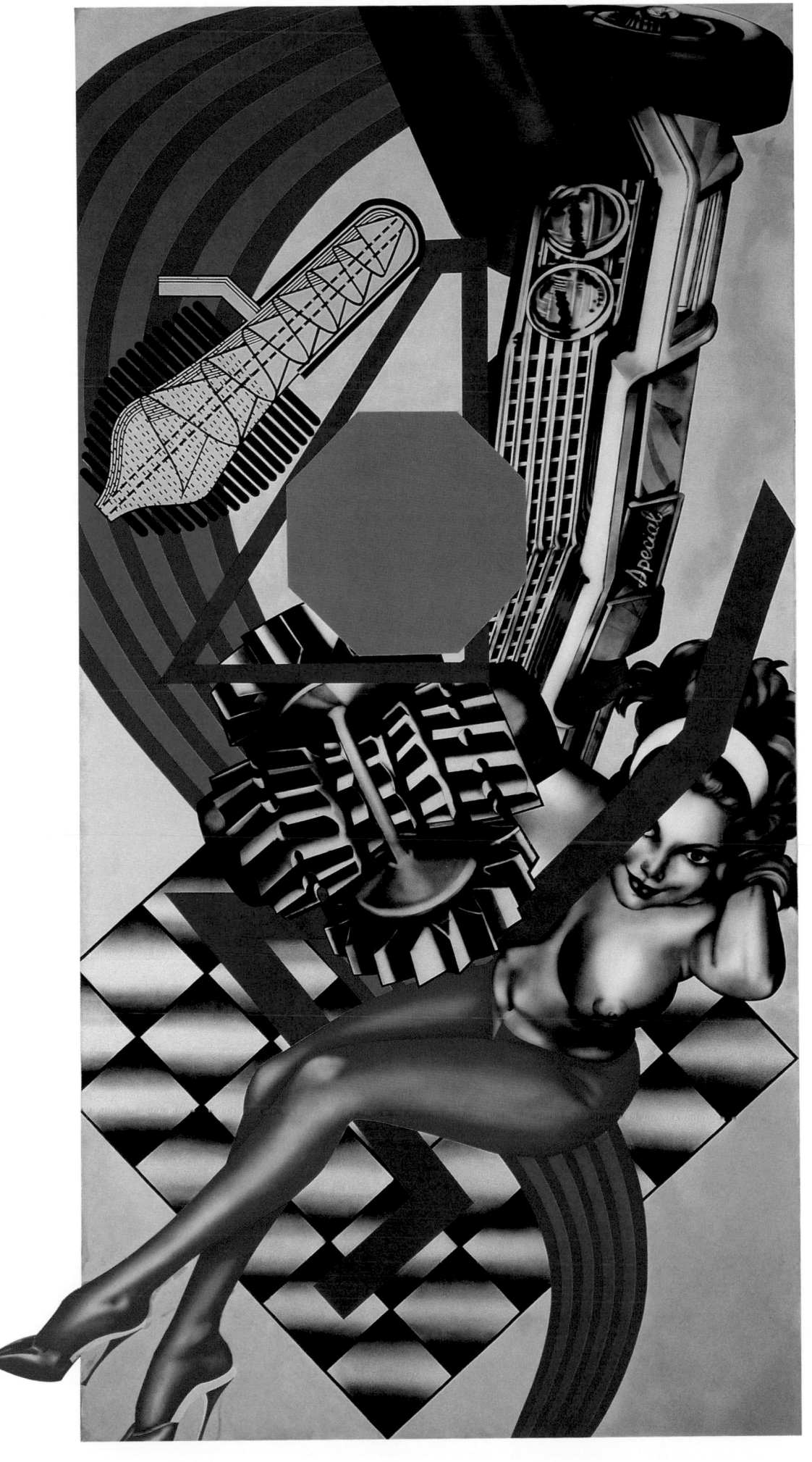

38

Claes Oldenburg (1929–)
Shoestring Potatoes Spilling from a Bag

1965–6. Canvas filled with kapok, painted with glue and Liquitex,
269.2 x 116.8 x 106.7 cm. Walker Art Center, Minneapolis

In 1963, Oldenburg turned to soft sculptures, the form with which he was most strongly identified throughout the heyday of Pop Art in the 1960s. The first of these was a soft pay telephone, constructed from shiny black vinyl and partially stuffed with kapok, so that it seemed to be melting. Other works, such as *Ghost Drum Set* (Private collection), were constructed from canvas and left unstuffed, so that the final work was a mystifying heap of tailored cloth, unidentifiable except from the work's title. Oldenburg's wife, Coosje van Bruggen, who was a skilled seamstress, was his collaborator on the soft sculptures. *Shoestring Potatoes Spilling from a Bag* is an important work, for it shows the artist's growing interest in monumental scale. Gravity, traditionally the sculptor's enemy, is here enlisted as an ally, to bring the luridly painted 'shoestring potatoes' cascading down around the viewer's head. By the late 1960s, Oldenburg was one of the most successful and influential artists to emerge from the Pop Art movement. He has received many commissions for public sculptures, such as a giant baseball bat which stands in front of Yankee Stadium, in New York City.

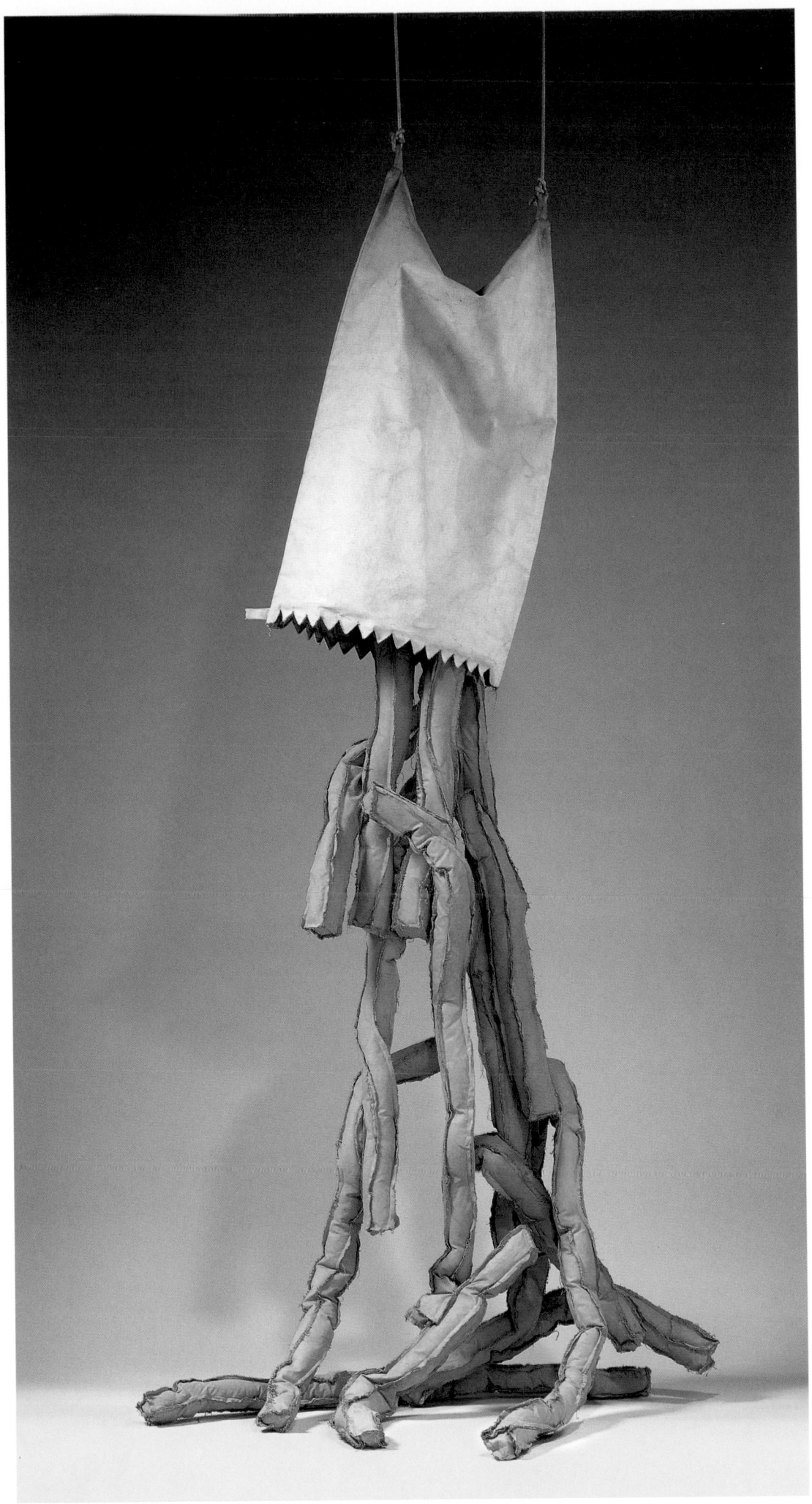

39

ED RUSCHA (1937–)
The Los Angeles County Museum of Art on Fire

1965–8. Oil on canvas, 135.9 x 339.1 cm. Hirshhorn Museum, Smithsonian Institution, Washington DC

In the early 1960s, Ruscha painted several paintings of fires, including this one of the Los Angeles County Museum of Art, the city's principal art institution. The perspective of the painting follows the bold, almost vertiginous diagonal of his word paintings, such as *Twentieth-Century Fox with Searchlights* (Fig. 24). The aerial perspective, which suggests a crane shot in a big-budget Hollywood epic, reduces the museum to the scale of an architectural model. The painting is a savagely witty piece of satire, drawing the viewer into an art-world inside joke. While one might expect that the artist would harbour an ambition to be exhibited at the museum, he here openly expresses a violent fantasy that many an aspiring artist has had: the desire to see the whole place go up in smoke. The work seems to imply that for all its pretensions, the museum is as vapid and characterless as a gas station (another of Ruscha's fire paintings showed a Standard Oil station engulfed in flames). The style of the painting is cool and understated; the viewer senses that Ruscha would like the museum even less if it had more character.

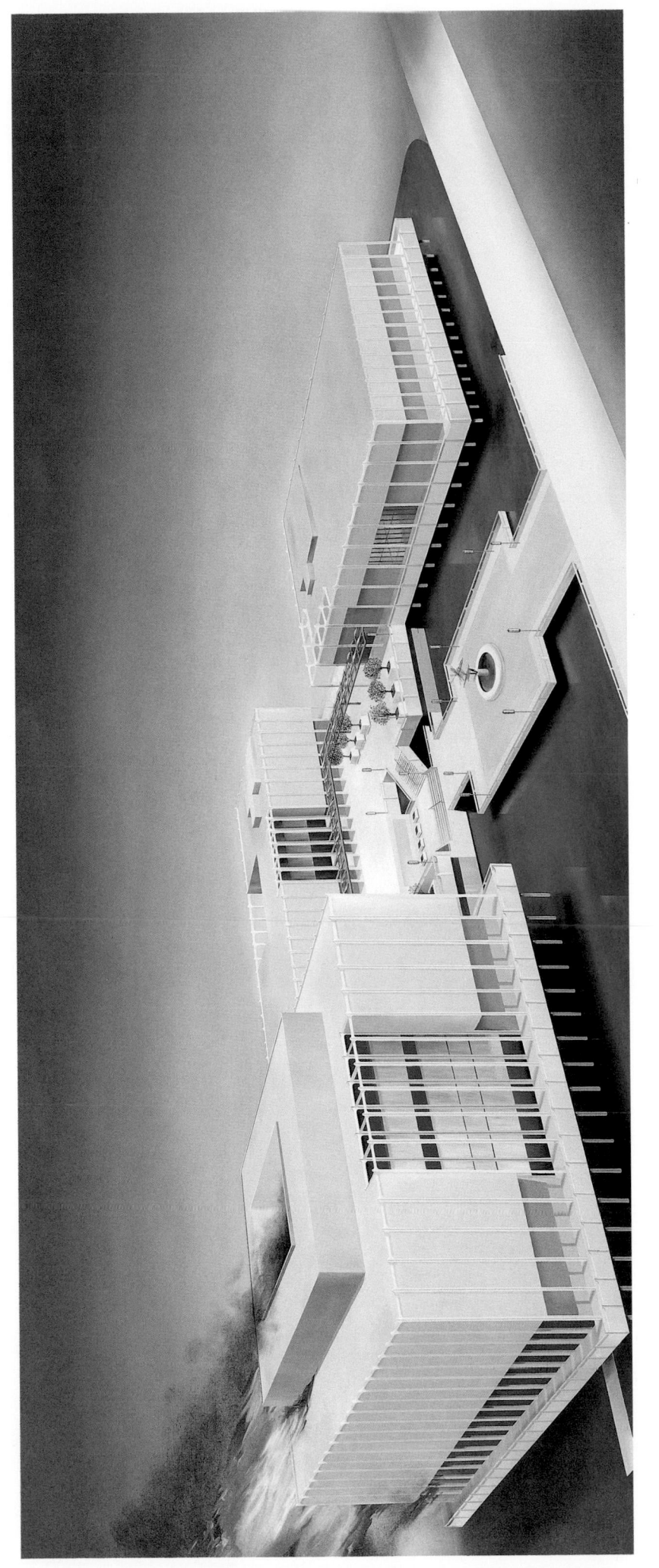

40

SIGMAR POLKE (1941–)
Rasterbild mit Palmen
(Screen Painting with Palms)

1966. Oil on canvas, 130 x 110 cm. Private collection

The most successful European artists working in the Pop Art idiom are both German: Sigmar Polke and Gerhard Richter. This early canvas by Polke neatly combines stylistic elements of two leading Americans: his glaring, slightly off-register colour suggests the silk-screen paintings of Andy Warhol, while the prominent use of Ben-Day dots invokes the comic-strip paintings of Roy Lichtenstein. Yet the painting's cool subject-matter, an indistinct, idealized North African landscape, seems closer in spirit to the British Pop artist Patrick Caulfield, whose *Christ at Emmaus* (Plate 22) also makes conspicuous use of a palm-tree motif. Like Caulfield, Polke rejected American iconography, and many of his later paintings have a strong political undercurrent. The American war in Vietnam was expanding rapidly at the time, and the intellectual currents in Europe were growing more and more anti-American. Whereas Andy Warhol was able to paint pictures of race riots and atomic bomb explosions and yet proclaim, however ironically, his love of America and its popular culture, Polke and Richter, as members of the European intelligentsia, were decidedly hostile in their view of the American influence. Richter's *Eight Student Nurses* (Fig. 25) is a group of portraits of the victims of mass murderer Richard Speck in Chicago, one of the most notorious American criminals in the 1960s. Although the figures are hand-painted, their appearance is almost indistinguishable from Warhol's silkscreened paintings. And while the tone is complex and highly intellectualized, at the time their implicit condemnation of America was clear enough to a European audience.

Fig. 25
GERHARD RICHTER
Eight Student Nurses
1966. Oil on canvas,
94.9 x 69.9 cm.
Private collection

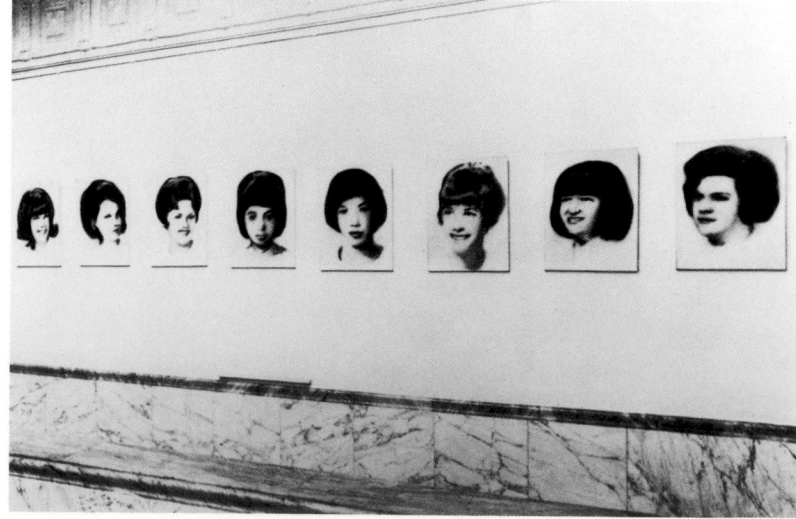

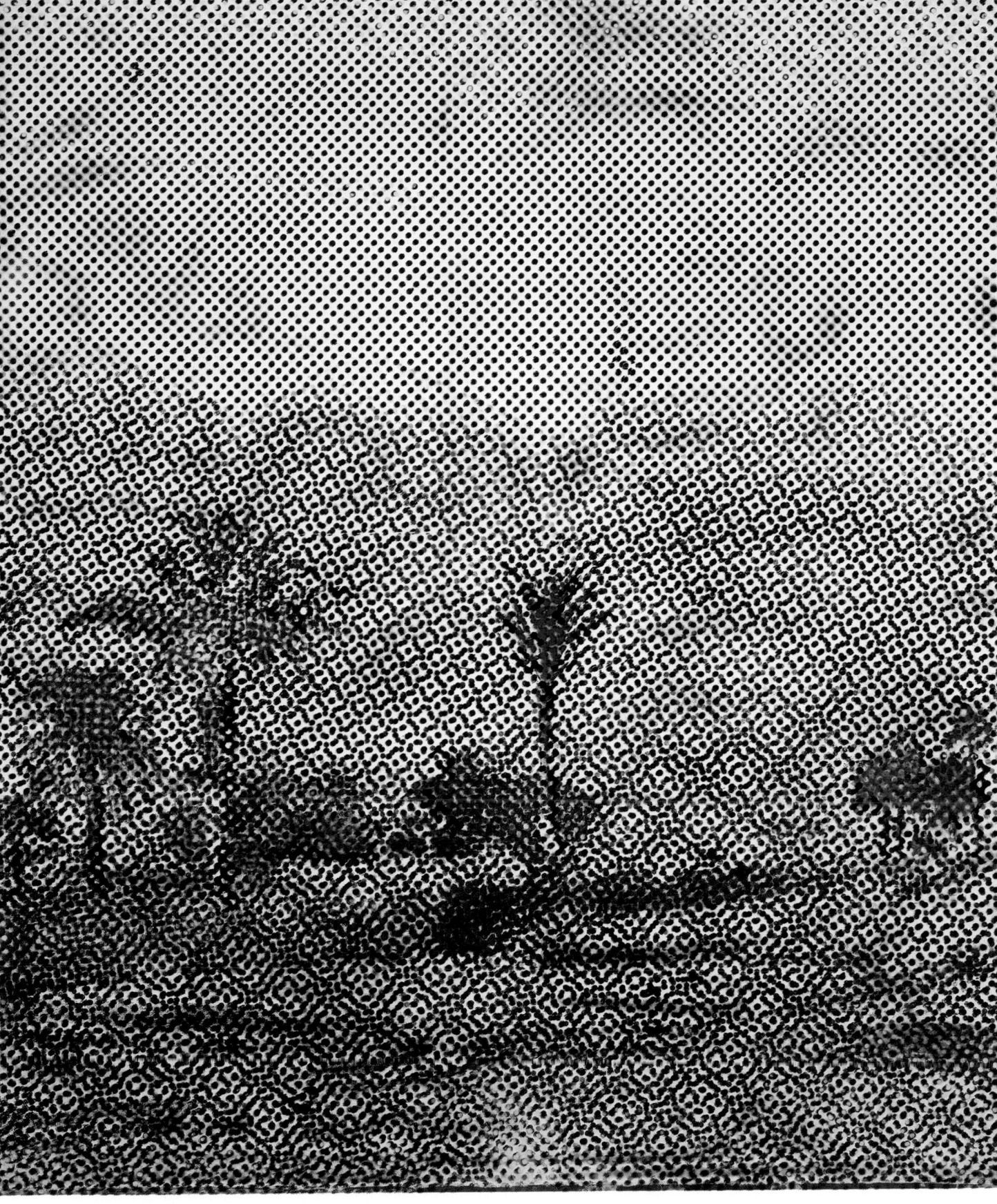

41

ANDY WARHOL (1926–86)
Self-portrait

1967. Synthetic polymer paint silkscreened on canvas, 183 x 183 cm. Tate Gallery, London

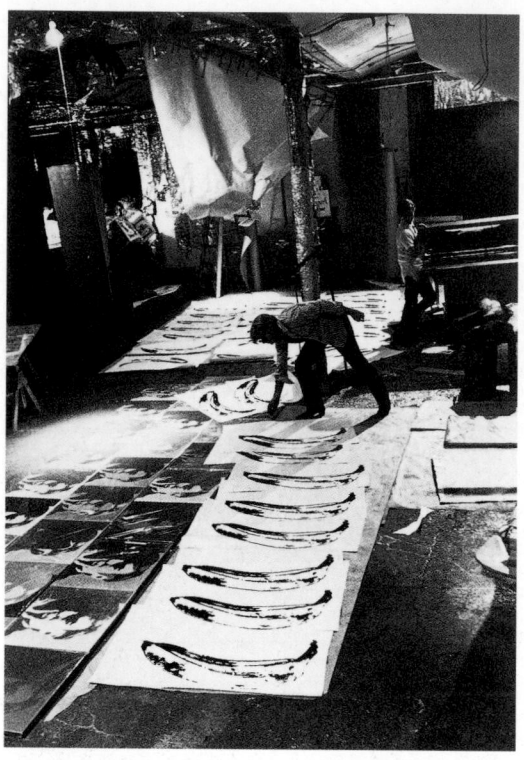

Fig. 26
BILLY NAME
Photograph of Andy
Warhol at the Factory
with self-portraits and
large bananas, 1966

In the later years of his career, Warhol concentrated more and more on portraiture. Probably the most famous and financially successful artist America has yet produced, Warhol was also an assiduous social climber and 'hobnobber'; he chronicled his career as a socialite in great detail in his posthumously published *Diaries*. Some of his best portraits were *hommages* to people he admired; many of them are of pop stars such as Mick Jagger and Grace Jones, or of other artists, including Rauschenberg and Joseph Beuys (1921–86). However, a great many of his portraits were commissioned by the wealthy people Warhol met on his social rounds. In his socializing he was only following the long-standing tradition, and perhaps necessity, for the portraitist to mix socially with his patrons. Many of these portraits were commissioned by the subjects, and are rarely exhibited. Pursuing another long-standing tradition in Western art, Warhol's favourite subject in his portraiture, a figure as rich and famous as any of them, was himself: he created self-portraits frequently throughout his career. This cool, characteristic self-portrait became one of the defining images of the Pop Art movement and indeed of the 1960s.

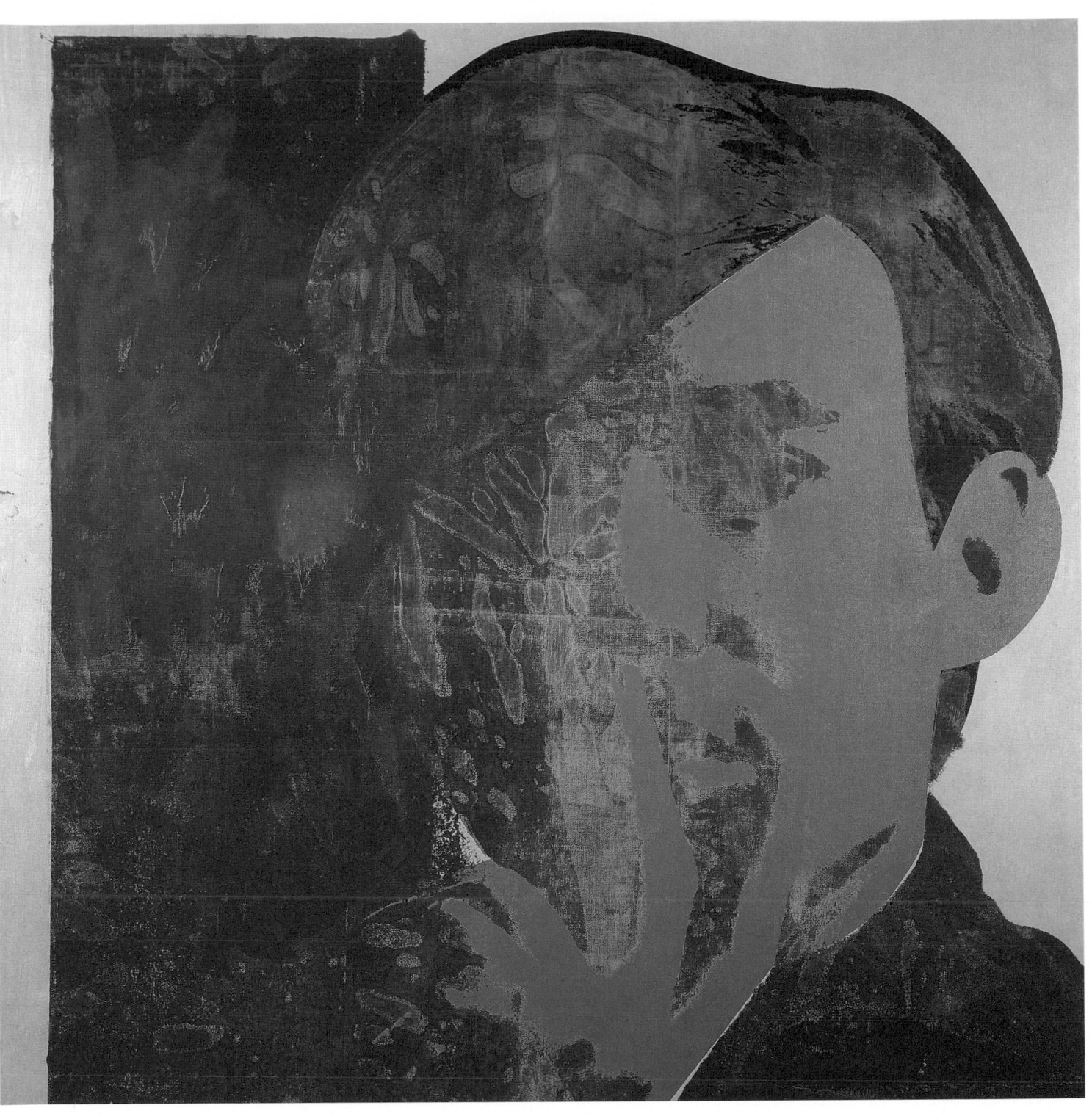

42

ROY LICHTENSTEIN (1923–)
Haystacks

1968. Oil and magna on canvas, 45.7 x 61 cm. Tate Gallery, London

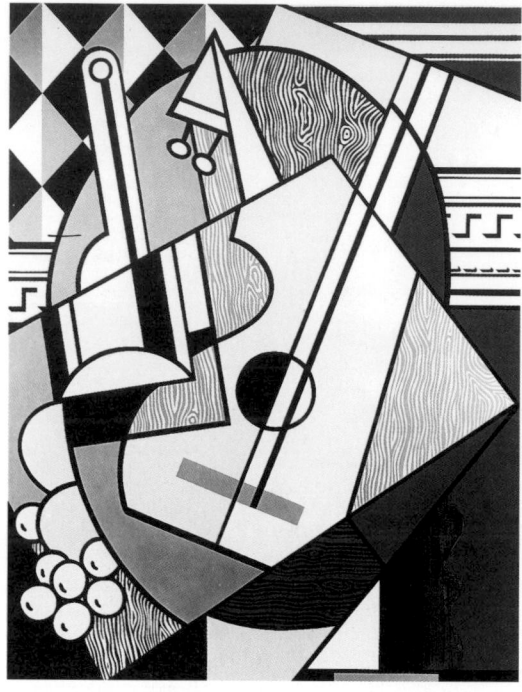

Fig. 27
ROY LICHTENSTEIN
Cubist Still Life
1974. Oil and magna on
canvas, 228.6 x 173.2 cm.
National Gallery of Art,
Washington DC

Fig. 28
CLAUDE MONET
Haystacks in Winter
1891. Oil on canvas, 65.4 x
92.3 cm. Museum of Fine
Arts, Boston

Almost from the very beginning of his career, Lichtenstein produced canvases in which he applied the bold graphic style of his comic-strip paintings to compositions borrowed from famous works of art. Paintings by Picasso (1881–1973), Cézanne (1839–1906), and, in this case, Monet (1840–1926) (Fig. 28), were reduced to their most basic compositional elements, and then rendered using crude printing techniques. These paintings were even more radical and inflammatory than the ones based upon comic strips, for they implied an equivalency between some of the most revered works of modern art and the disposable, banal trash designed for and read by adolescents. The results are particularly striking in the case of the Monet; for while the composition of a Cézanne painting and the Cubist vision of a work by Picasso survive the Lichtenstein treatment, albeit in a debased, rudimentary form, the essence of Monet's painting – the evanescent light, the subtle modulations of colour, the delicate brushwork – have all disappeared in the Lichtenstein version, replaced by harsh grids of flat colour.

This painting also raises an interesting question about the definition of Pop Art, which in the beginning was usually defined as fine art that borrowed its imagery from mass consumer culture. That definition clearly does not apply to a work based on Monet or Leonardo da Vinci, whose *Mona Lisa* (Musée du Louvre, Paris) Andy Warhol used in several of his early silkscreened paintings. Because the two most prominent (and most indisputably Pop) painters of the group expanded their repertory of images beyond the consumer culture, Pop Art also came to include any art that borrowed the techniques of commercial art, regardless of the subject-matter. In his later career Lichtenstein painted images drawn from a multitude of fine-art sources, including some that were completely invented, such as the idealized *Cubist Still Life* (Fig. 27) of 1974. By then, there was little doubt about what Pop Art was – or that Lichtenstein was it.

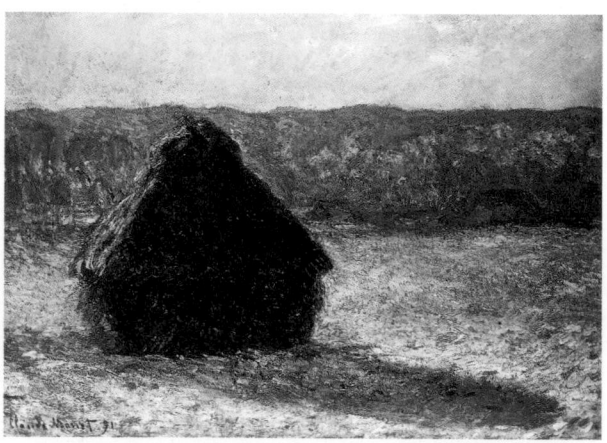

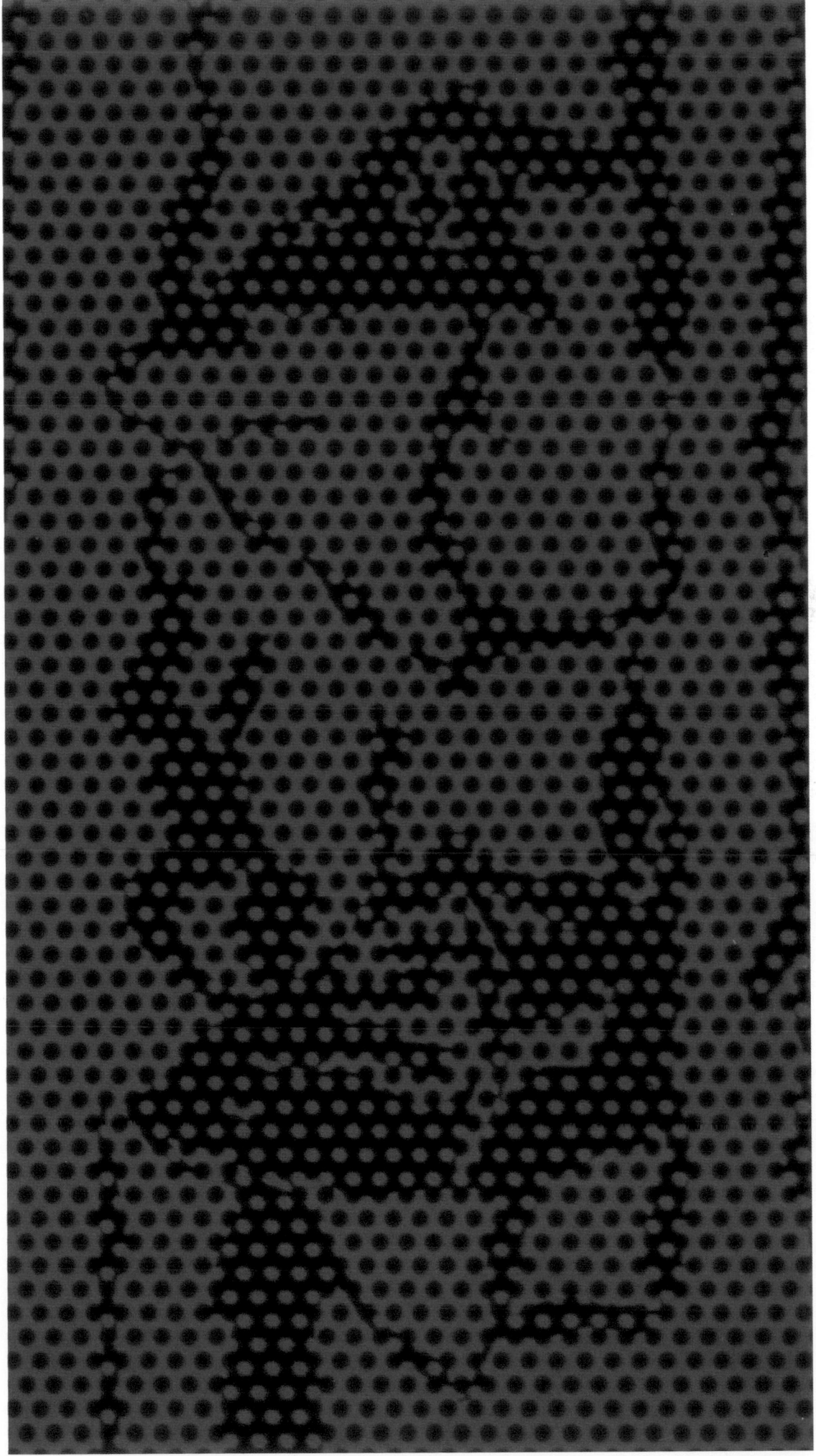

43

CINDY SHERMAN (1954–)
Untitled Film Still #21

1978. Black and white photograph, 40.6 x 50.8 cm. Saatchi Collection, London

Hollywood provided a rich source of imagery for Pop artists throughout the 1960s. Warhol was the most famous purveyor of images of movie stars; and while most of these were portraits, early in his career he also did a few paintings based upon Hollywood film stills, using films such as *Dracula*, *The Wild One* and others. Later, of course, Warhol made his own movies. Film imagery also appears in the work of many other Pop artists, particularly the movement's early exponents in Britain. Cindy Sherman is one of the most successful of the second-generation Pop artists in New York. Her earliest works, the black-and-white *Untitled Film Stills* series, were based upon the *film noir* of Hollywood B movies from the 1950s and early 1960s. She created single images from imagined 'films', casting herself as the heroine. The situations typically made a sexual-political point, portraying the woman in the picture either as a peroxide-blonde vixen or as a helpless, frightened victim; in *Untitled Film Still #21*, she invokes the stereotype of the naive girl from a small town, lost in the Big City. Sherman's photographs were made in locations that were carefully contrived to resemble the sets of the cheap movies she was simulating, but the rough edges were frequently left visible; occasionally the cord leading to the remote shutter in her hand may be clearly seen.

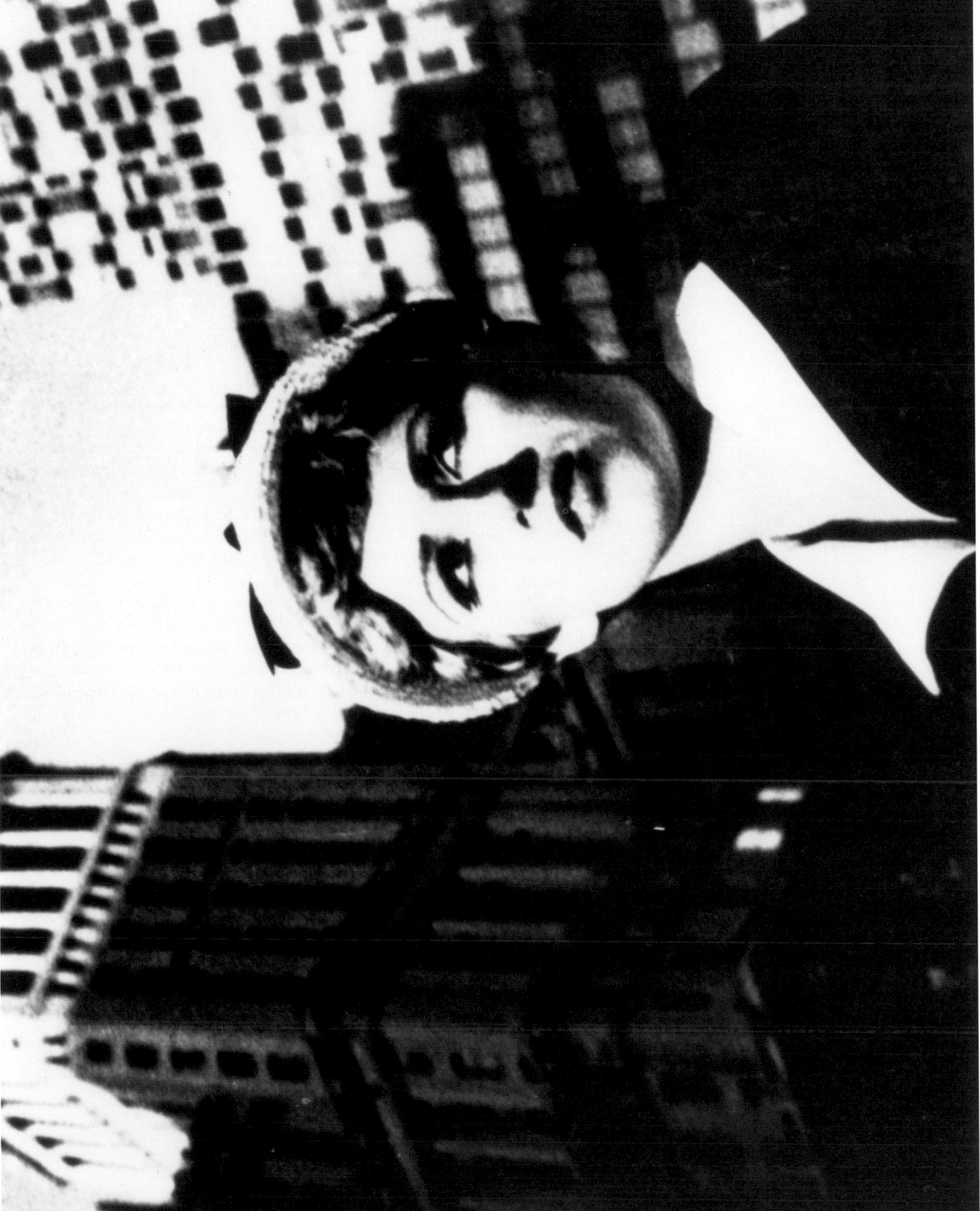

44

KENNY SCHARF (1958–)
Felix on a Pedestal

1982. Acrylic and spray paint on canvas, 243.8 x 264 cm. Private collection

Kenny Scharf met Keith Haring in 1978 at the School of Visual Arts in New York, where they were both students. The two became close friends and worked together often. They frequented a nightclub in the East Village called Club 57, an informal (and illegal) bar housed in the basement of a Polish church and run by a performance artist named Ann Magnuson. The room had a small stage, where Haring, Scharf and other art students and demimonde hangers-on staged raucous poetry readings and spontaneous evenings of cabaret. The Club 57 scene was bright, colourful, silly and anarchic in a style that was perhaps closer to the Dadaist Cabaret Voltaire than to the Happenings of Claes Oldenburg and Jim Dine. Influenced by Haring, Scharf began to create art using spray paint, in the style of the graffiti artists who were painting the subway trains in New York at that time. In addition to drawings and paintings, Scharf also made a large number of what he called 'customized appliances', ordinary household appliances such as telephones, blenders and television sets, which were covered with images in the graffiti style. Whereas Haring's style was reduced to bare, bold outlines, Scharf favoured highly finished paintings of what he described as 'super-realistic images of things you couldn't photograph, like objects from outer space. It was all imaginary subject matter which I'd paint in a photo-realistic way.' *Felix on a Pedestal* makes a pointed reference to the Pop Art of the early 1960s by including the figure of Felix the Cat, a popular American comic-strip character.

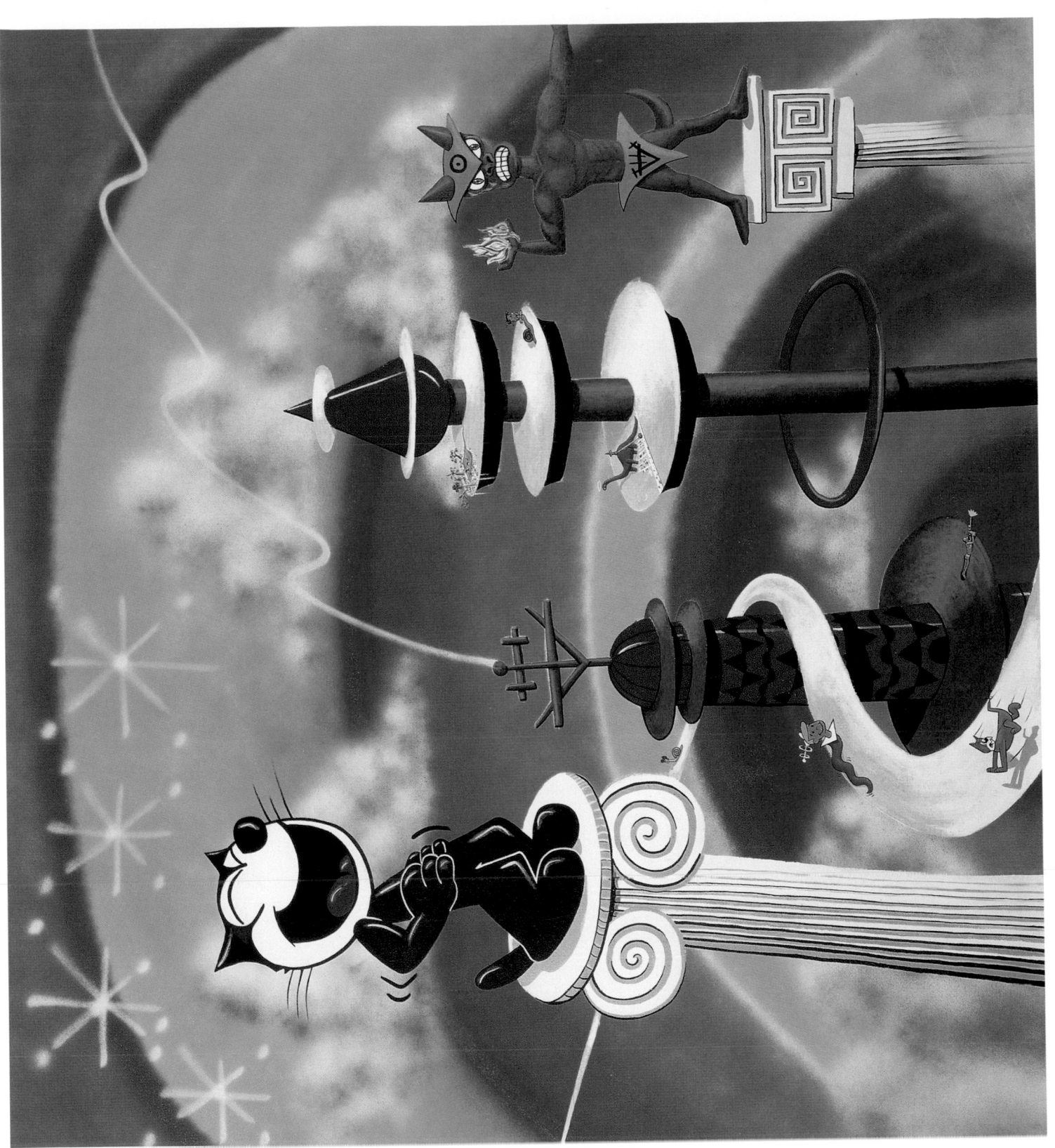

45

KEITH HARING (1958–90)
Cruella De Ville

1985. Acrylic on canvas, 152.4 x 152.4 cm. Private collection

This American graffiti artist epitomized the outlaw lifestyle of New York's East Village in the high-living 1970s and early 1980s. Haring originally became known for his chalk and spray paint art, which he executed on the city's streets and sidewalks. After his first one-man exhibition at the Tony Shafrazi Gallery in 1983, he was established almost literally overnight as one of the art world's biggest celebrities; he became a close friend of Andy Warhol's, and Madonna sang at his twenty-sixth birthday party. The day that he met Keith Haring, Henry Geldzahler, the former curator of contemporary art at the Metropolitan Museum of Art and later the parks commissioner of the City of New York, announced to his staff that Haring was a genius, and urged them all to go out and buy his paintings. Haring's style combined the frenetic energy and bizarre inventiveness of New York street art with a facile mimicry of the modernist idiom. Some critics question whether he really ought to be regarded as a Pop artist, since the vast majority of his images are self-invented. Nonetheless, he did borrow from pop culture occasionally, as here. Cruella De Ville, who appears in the Walt Disney cartoon *101 Dalmatians*, is an evil character who tries to make a fur coat from the pelts of a litter of puppies. In Haring's painting, however, she resembles a female figure in a late Picasso painting rather than Disney's campy villainess.

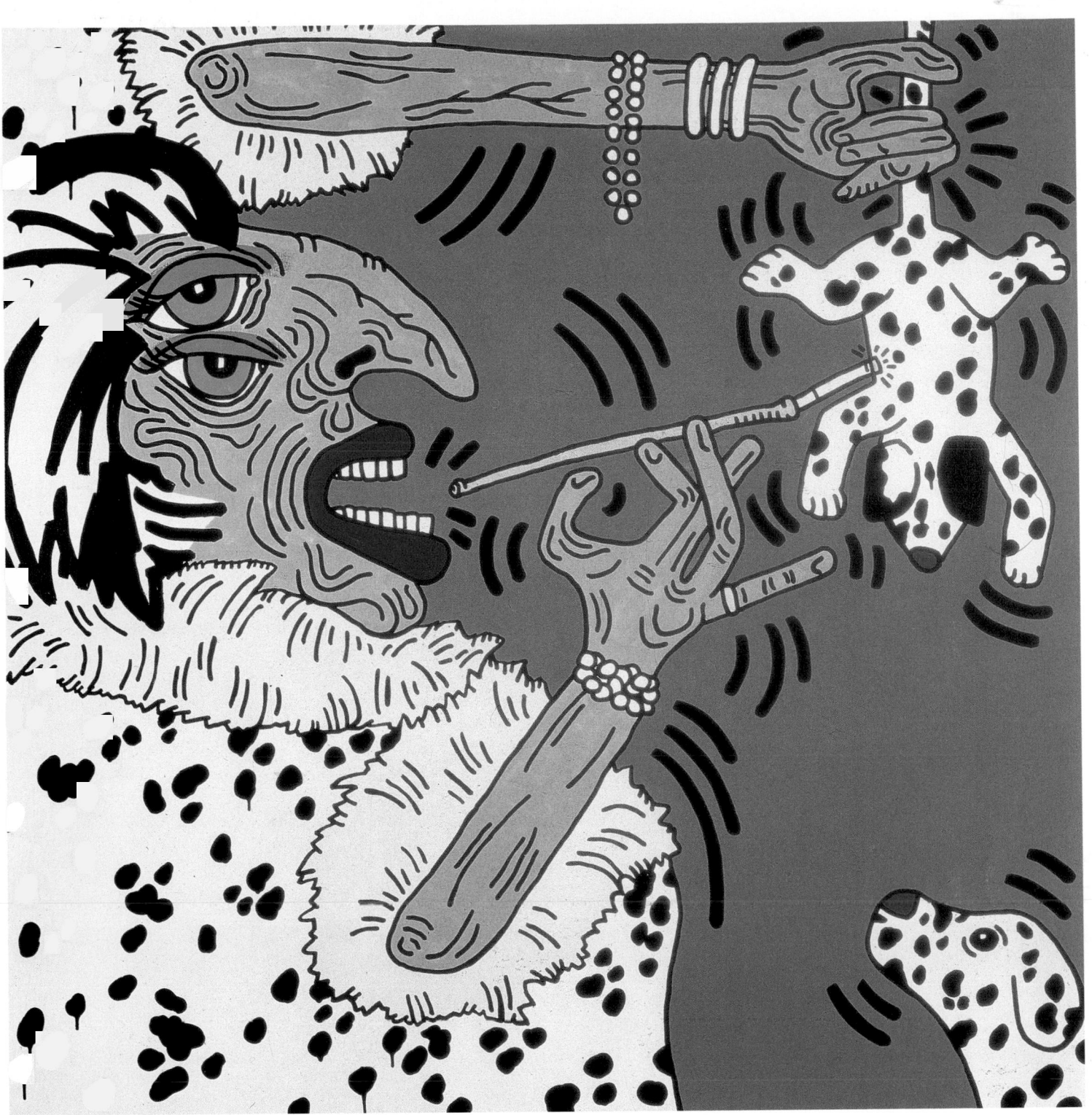

46

KEITH HARING (1958–90)
Andy Mouse

1985. Acrylic on canvas, 152.4 x 152.4 cm. Private collection

By 1983 Andy Warhol had become the undisputed king of the art world in New York, and Keith Haring was his chief acolyte. The two met at the opening of a show of Haring's at the Fun Gallery. They soon became close friends and were often seen together at the city's hippest nightclubs. They even collaborated on a number of works. *Madonna: 'I'm Not Ashamed'* (Fig. 18) is based upon a real newspaper headline, which the two artists transformed in their characteristic styles. *Andy Mouse*, Haring's affectionate caricature of the older artist as Mickey Mouse, is a typically quirky brainstorm. Although Andy Warhol never made a painting of Mickey Mouse, and had indeed only made a very few early, tentative canvases of comic-book subjects, it was a natural association to make between the King of Pop and the most popular cartoon character in the world. The irony of seeing Andy Warhol, an artist who scarcely ever touched a paint brush, with one dripping in his hand, would be apparent to anyone viewing the work.

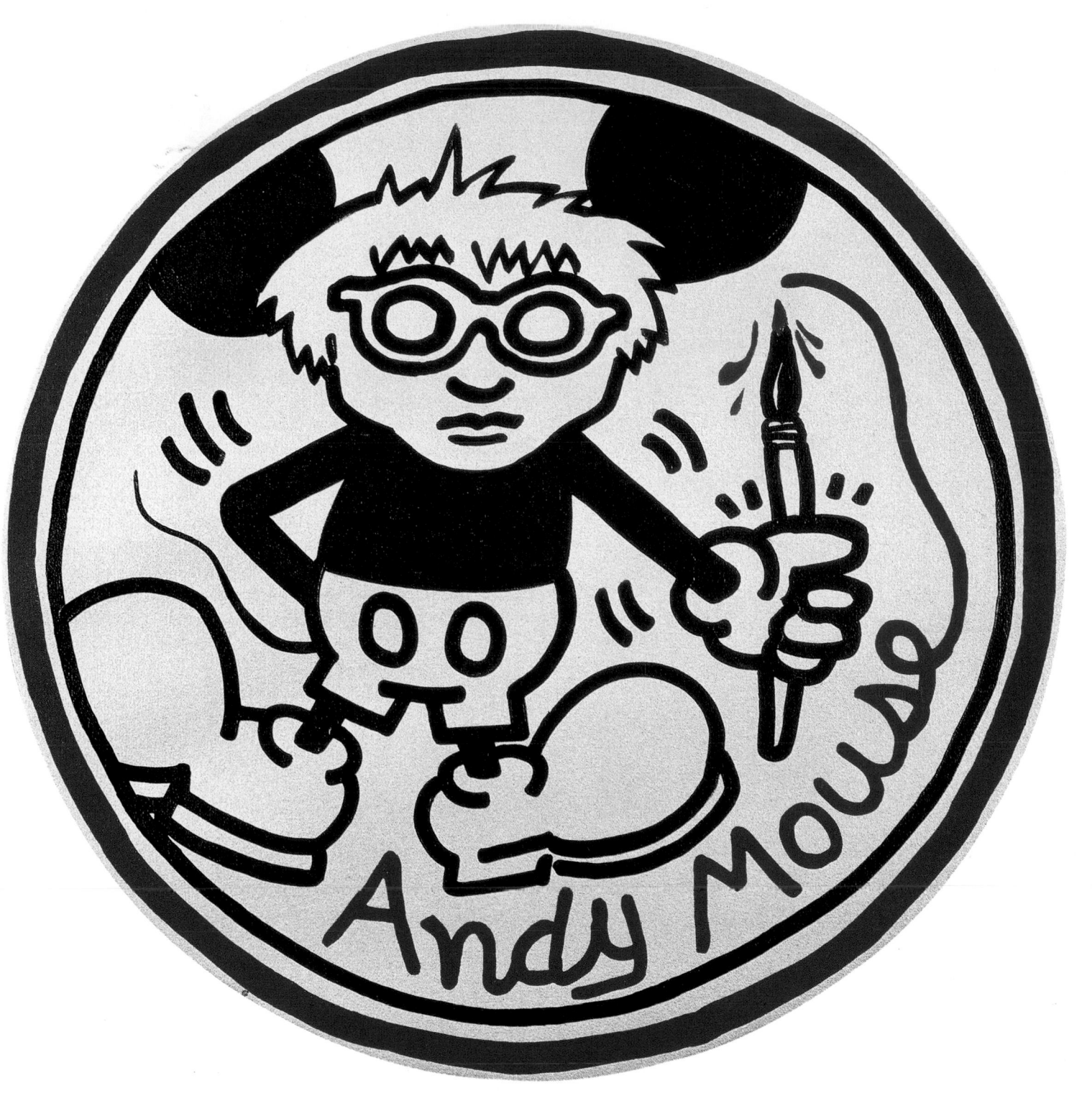

47

JEFF KOONS (1955–)
Yorkshire Terriers

1991. Polychromed wood, 41 x 48 x 39.8 cm. Private collection

For artists who grew up in an era when Warhol and Hockney were household names, Pop Art was as much an established school of art as Impressionism, Cubism, or any other ism that had preceded it. Many of these younger artists have used the forms of Pop Art to make statements which reflect their own concerns. Jeff Koons sees American consumer culture not merely as a source of imagery but as a source of liberation. He embraces the banal with a fervour that is quite different from the cool attitude of Rosenquist, Lichtenstein or Warhol. Most of his early works consist of commercial objects absurdly juxtaposed, very much in the spirit of Marcel Duchamp's readymades: basketballs bobbing in an aquarium, a Hoover vacuum cleaner in a plastic box lit with fluorescent light tubes. Whereas Pop artists in the 1960s took high art, paintings by Leonardo da Vinci and Claude Monet, and then cheapened them by using deliberately crude techniques and mindless repetition (see Plate 42), Koons in more recent work has taken cheap, ugly objects and tastelessly elevated them to high art. Here an aggressively hideous statue of dogs is, in its own way, far more insidious than were Warhol's Campbell's soup cans and Coca-Cola bottles. Warhol, at least in part, was motivated to choose the Campbell's cans and Coca-Cola bottles because they were well-designed, but Koons is attracted to the dogs' ugliness. Koons is a highly controversial figure; in 1991 he exhibited photographs and highly finished crystal sculptures of himself engaging in unusual sex acts with his wife.

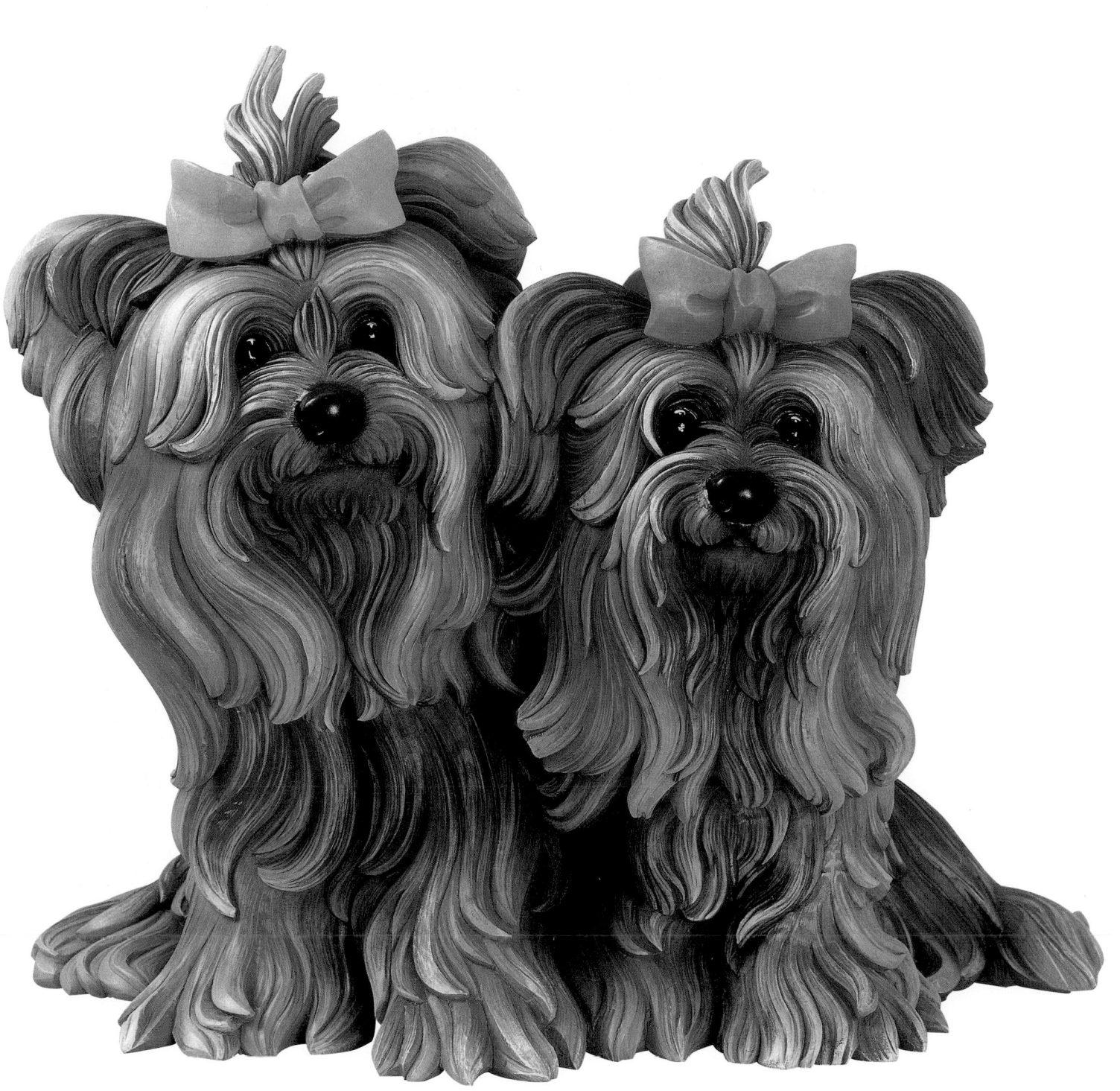

48

Deborah Kass (1952–)
Sixteen Barbras (The Jewish Jackie Series)

1992. Silkscreen ink on acrylic on canvas, 152.4 x 182.8 cm. Private collection

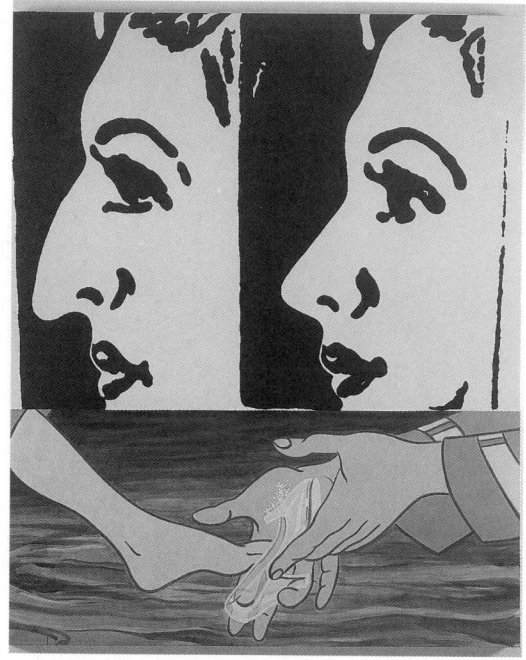

Fig. 29
Deborah Kass
Before and Happily
Ever After
1991. Acrylic and oil on
canvas, 182.9 x 152.4 cm.
Private collection

By the time of his death, in 1986, Andy Warhol was one of the most famous and widely revered artists in America. His bold graphic style was widely imitated by younger artists, as well as by commercial designers. While many among the younger generation of Pop artists in New York have made explicit reference to Warhol's work, Deborah Kass has gone one step further, modelling an entire career on his. Her early works were landscapes and abstract compositions, but by the late 1980s she was painting canvases that combined disparate art historical references. In 1991 she began to appropriate images and concepts from Warhol paintings, reinterpreting them in the light of her own identity as a feminist Jewish lesbian.

Kass's first 'Warhol', *Before and Happily Ever After* (Fig. 29), was based upon a work Andy Warhol created in 1960 for a window display at a department store in New York. *Before and After* was derived from a newspaper advertisement for a plastic surgeon, which showed a woman with a large, hooked nose ('before') and, transformed by surgery, with a small nose ('after'). Kass combined this image with the scene from Walt Disney's *Cinderella* in which Prince Charming fits the glass slipper onto the heroine's foot: girls with small noses, it seems, have more successful love lifes.

In *Sixteen Barbras*, Kass alludes to Warhol's serial portraits of Jacqueline Kennedy, Marilyn Monroe, and other famous figures, but she has chosen her own, personal heroine – the pop singer Barbra Streisand, a Jewish woman with a famously large, hooked nose. In other works, Kass has reimagined some of Warhol's best known paintings, substituting female subjects for the men in the originals: Barbra Streisand (in the title role of her film *Yentl*) as Elvis Presley, a portrait of Gertrude Stein and Alice B. Toklas entitled *Let Us Now Praise Famous Women* (Private collection), patterned after Warhol's *Let Us Now Praise Famous Men* (Private collection), a portrait of Robert Rauschenberg and his family.

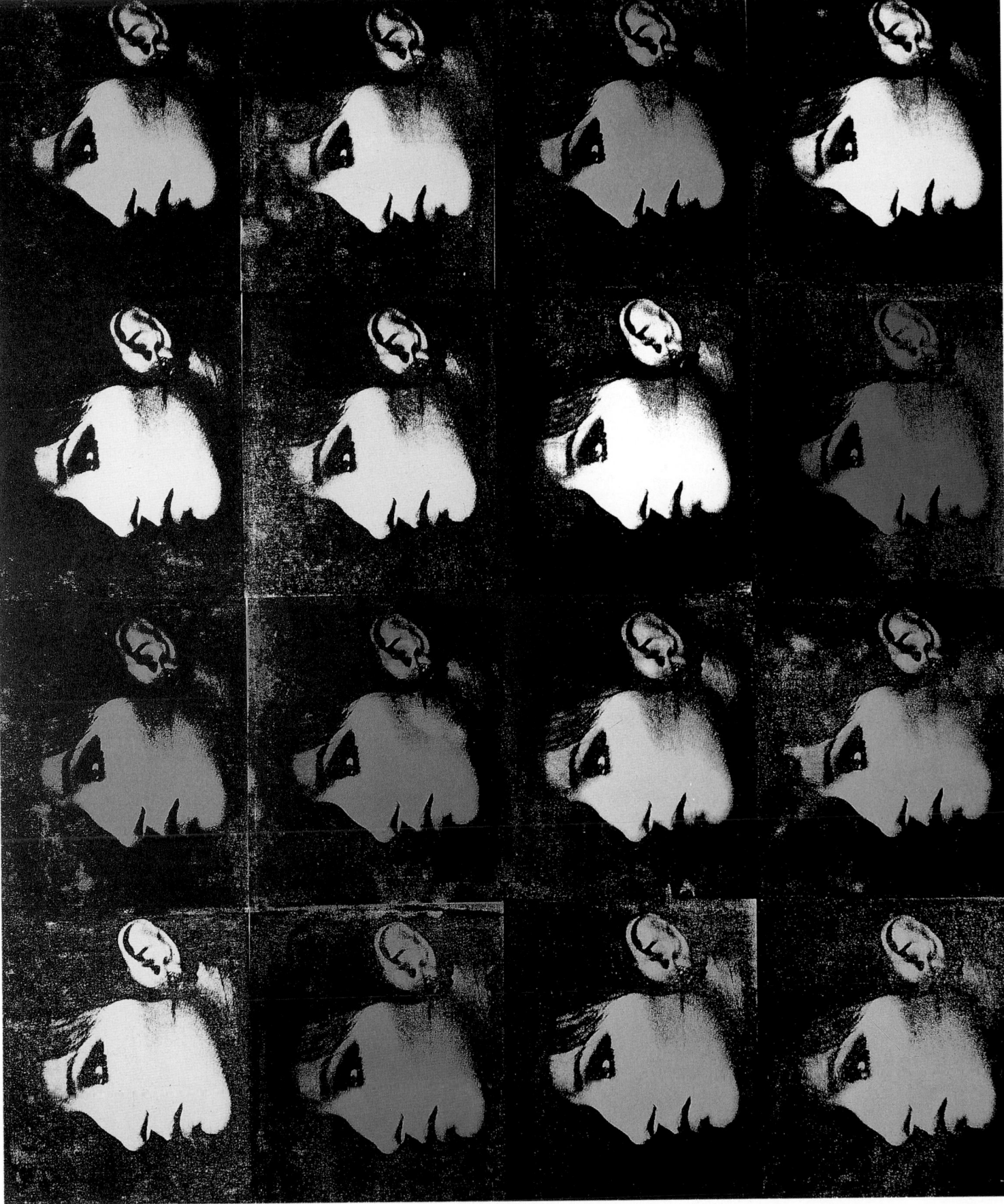

PHAIDON COLOUR LIBRARY
Titles in the series

 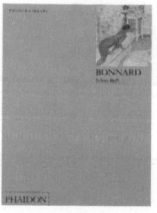 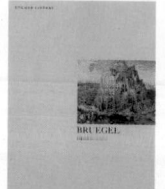 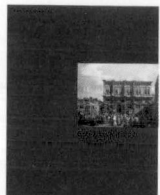 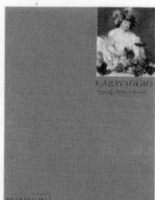  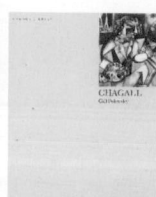 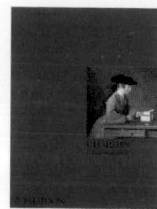 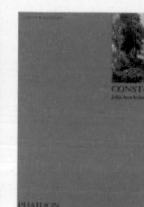

FRA ANGELICO
Christopher Lloyd

BONNARD
Julian Bell

BRUEGEL
Keith Roberts

CANALETTO
Christopher Baker

CARAVAGGIO
Timothy
Wilson-Smith

CEZANNE
Catherine Dean

CHAGALL
Gill Polonsky

CHARDIN
Gabriel Naughton

CONSTABLE
John Sunderland

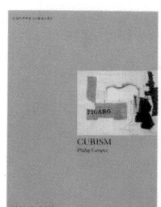 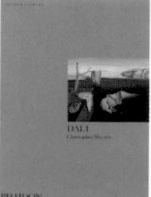 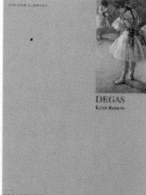 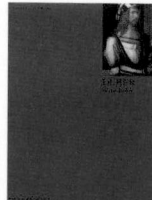 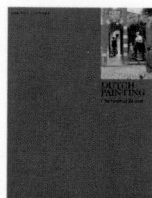 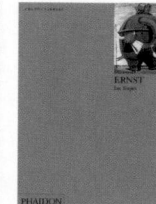 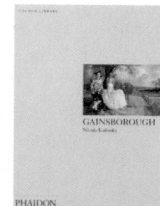 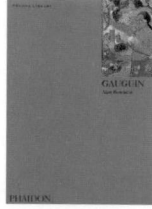 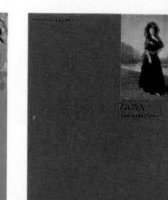

CUBISM
Philip Cooper

DALÍ
Christopher Masters

DEGAS
Keith Roberts

DÜRER
Martin Bailey

DUTCH PAINTING
Christopher Brown

ERNST
Ian Turpin

GAINSBOROUGH
Nicola Kalinsky

GAUGUIN
Alan Bowness

GOYA
Enriqueta Harris

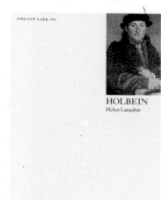 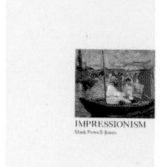 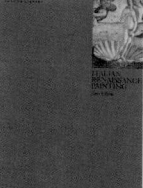 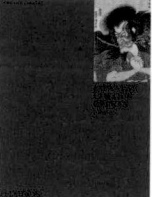 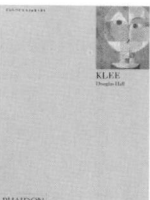 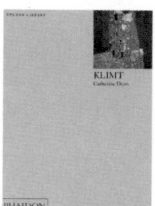 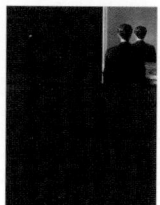 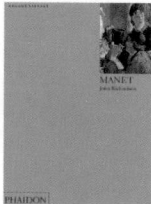 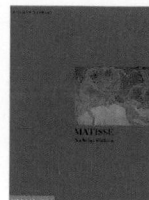

HOLBEIN
Helen Langdon

IMPRESSIONISM
Mark Powell-Jones

**ITALIAN
RENAISSANCE
PAINTING**
Sara Elliott

**JAPANESE
COLOUR PRINTS**
J. Hillier

KLEE
Douglas Hall

KLIMT
Catherine Dean

MAGRITTE
Richard Calvocoressi

MANET
John Richardson

MATISSE
Nicholas Watkins

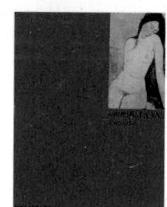 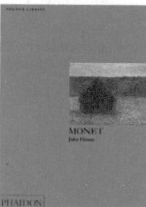 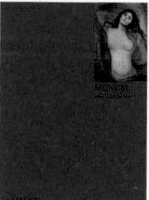 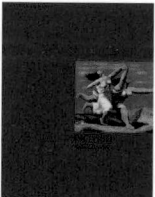 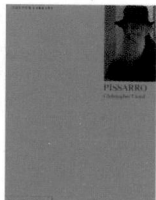 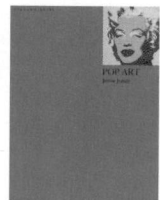 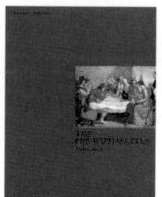 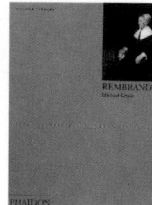 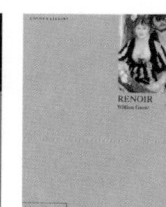

MODIGLIANI
Douglas Hall

MONET
John House

MUNCH
John Boulton Smith

PICASSO
Roland Penrose

PISSARRO
Christopher Lloyd

POP ART
Jamie James

**THE PRE-
RAPHAELITES**
Andrea Rose

REMBRANDT
Michael Kitson

RENOIR
William Gaunt

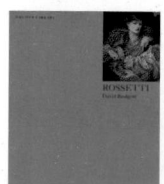 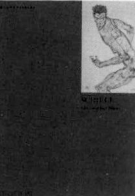 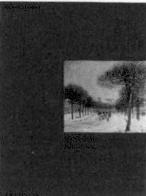 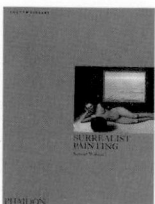 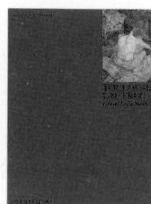  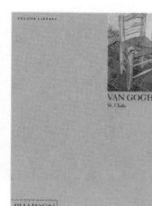 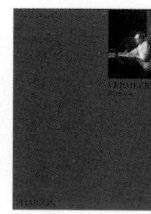 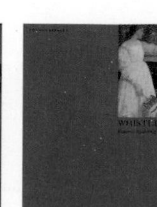

ROSSETTI
David Rodgers

SCHIELE
Christopher Short

SISLEY
Richard Shone

**SURREALIST
PAINTING**
Simon Wilson

**TOULOUSE-
LAUTREC**
Edward Lucie-Smith

TURNER
William Gaunt

VAN GOGH
Wilhelm Uhde

VERMEER
Martin Bailey

WHISTLER
Frances Spalding